SOUTHERN JOURNEYS

Other books by Roy Sinclair:

The Spirit of Steam and Rail
The Great New Zealand Adventure
New Zealand Aviation Yarns
Journeying with Railways
Journeying with Aviators
Journeying with Seafarers

SOUTHERN JOURNEYS

SOUTH ISLAND PEOPLE AND PLACES

ROY SINCLAIR

RANDOM HOUSE
NEW ZEALAND

ACKNOWLEDGEMENTS

As always, many people helped to originate these stories collected during many South Island journeys, adventures and a few misadventures. Gordon Burrow of YHA New Zealand ensured I never had to sleep under a bridge, or in a bus shelter. The standard of YHA backpacking accommodation is simply incredible, and I was often treated to the best of it.

Tranz Rail's Tranz Scenic, and especially the South Island manager Darin Cusack, ensured I did not need to do a return bike ride across the South Island in December 1999.

And thanks to John Hurley, Mayor of the Tasman District Council, for introducing me to Gerald Tarrant, a one-time student of Ernest Rutherford.

A special thanks goes to Haruko Morita who accompanied me on some of these journeys and in return introduced me to her own special places in Japan.

Of course, the book could not have happened if South Island people had not taken the time to sit down and tell their stories. And there are those stories caught on the run; anyone recognising the incidents that inspired these pieces, will, I hope, be forgiving if my words have distorted the facts a tad.

A RANDOM HOUSE BOOK
published by
Random House New Zealand
18 Poland Road, Glenfield, Auckland, New Zealand
www.randomhouse.co.nz

First published 2001

© 2001 text and photographs Roy Sinclair

The moral rights of the author have been asserted

ISBN 1 86941 439 X

Design and layout: Kate Greenaway
Cover illustration: Roy Sinclair
Cover design: Eiméar Crawford
Printed by Publishing Press Ltd, Auckland

CONTENTS

Introduction 7

WESTWARD

CHAPTER 1   A Home for the Soul 12

CHAPTER 2   On Your Bike 24

CHAPTER 3   Hard-case Hotel 41

CHAPTER 4   Characters of the Coal Seams 47

CHAPTER 5   Hokitika's Seven Wonders 56
              Born to be Wild 62

CHAPTER 6   A Passion for Planes and Pizza 64

CLOSER TO HOME

CHAPTER 7   Defender of the Port Hills 72
              Heraldic Treasures 78

CHAPTER 8   Legends Among the Rocks 81

CHAPTER 9   Playing the Game 94

SOUTH

CHAPTER 10 Artist in the Mountains 108

CHAPTER 11 Chowbok of Erewhon 118

CHAPTER 12 Back Country Bard 126
Living on the Fringe 138

CHAPTER 13 The Luckiest Man in the Railway 142

NORTH

CHAPTER 14 Winning Ways with Wine 154

CHAPTER 15 Home is Where the Heart Is 165

CHAPTER 16 Tall Tales and Fine Fish 171

CHAPTER 17 Remembering Rutherford 181

CHAPTER 18 The Postmistress 195

Bibliography 204

INTRODUCTION

Driving in South Westland just a few days before the last Christmas of the twentieth century, I stopped with my companion for a cup of coffee at Harihari. A sleepy little town, it has nevertheless enjoyed its moments of excitement, the most cherished being the 1931 crash landing of the first solo trans-Tasman flight. Guy Menzies, a 21-year-old Sydneysider, had led newspaper reporters to believe he was flying non-stop to Perth, but on 6 January, at one o'clock in the morning, he took to the air in his Avro Avian G-ABCF 'Southern Cross' Junior and flew east towards New Zealand. In a little less than 12 hours he was over the South Island's West Coast, somewhat south of his anticipated landfall close to Greymouth. With cloud descending on the Southern Alps, the weary aviator decided to land near some houses in what appeared to be a small town.

Guy Menzies poses with his Junior Southern Cross, in Harihari in 1931, at the completion of the first solo trans-Tasman flight.

Menzies unceremoniously came to earth upside down, but unharmed, in La Fontaine Swamp near Harihari. Undoing his seat harness, he fell head-first the last few feet, completing his landing run with a baptism in mud. If his pride was slightly dampened in the mire it apparently did little to diminish his much-deserved hero's welcome by the town's inhabitants. Menzies subsequently joined the Royal Air Force but was posted missing over the Mediterranean in November 1940.

Menzies's story is undoubtedly the Harihari yarn of the century but, for me, the town will always be remembered for another, much smaller incident on that idyllic early summer morning late in 1999.

Close to where we were sipping coffee, a workman was up a ladder installing a new 'On the Spot' sign on the grocery store's verandah. His cheerful almost tuneful whistling could be heard between hammer blows. Before long he was greeted by a friend paying a mid-morning visit to the store. Looking up he said, 'Hi George. Great morning. Are you all ready for Father Christmas?'

George looked down and wryly replied, 'That miserable prick, he hasn't given me anything decent in years!'

George's retort brought a smile to my face. A few days before I had cycled from Christchurch to Greymouth in an effort to rediscover the trans-alpine route across the South Island at an appropriate pedaller's pace. As related elsewhere in this book, it was an exceptional experience that had, mercifully, enabled me to forget Christmas, less than two weeks away. I had locked my bike at the Greymouth Youth Hostel Association (YHA) and headed down the West Coast in a rental car. George's comment had brought me back to earth with a thud.

For all that, I would not expect to hear such a lack of reverence anywhere else in New Zealand. Could such words be spoken only in the South Island, and especially on the West Coast, a province that once set its own rules on drinking hours, and almost everything else?

This, of course, suggests that the South Island is different from the North Island. Indeed, no self-respecting one-eyed South Island would ever willingly become an Aucklander. He or she would never want to leave home, permanently, despite deplorable winters that all too often intrude into summer. So what is so great about the South Island?

For this unrepentant South Island writer it is a grandeur in landscape — and the people whose passions have made the South Island a special place. This book is a series of stories culminating in a single journey that has already lasted half a century and will, I hope, go on for a while yet.

The stories are about cherished places and equally cherished people. Some characters helped to shape my early life and form my many obsessions. Their contagious kindness and humour provided a panacea for all those forces hell bent on reducing my early life to its most dreary basics.

All the characters share a common interest: they have a passion for the South Island and talk with pride about the environments that form their backyards. Many, like me, were born here. Some are immigrants; others are merely visitors, passing through, but taking with them a little of the South Island's soul.

My association with some of the storytellers borders on the paradoxical. Hettie Feith-Wells, a delightful rockhound with a Dutch accent, arrived in New Zealand still reeling from terrible teenage experiences as a wartime prisoner of the Japanese in Indonesia. During the final 20 years of her colourful life she became a close friend and even asked me to tell some of her story and harsh experiences living under the daily threat of torture and death. Yet just days after Hettie died in November 1999 I scaled a mountain above Arthur's Pass with Haruko Morita, a delightful climbing companion from Japan. High above the clouds we discovered a common love for a special place that effectively bridged cultures and languages. Immigrant and visitor respectively, Hettie and Haruko both enhanced the South Island as my special place.

Looking to the north-west across the Canterbury Plains from the Port Hills a Cantabrian can appreciate the topography of the South Island. Bordering the plains is the line of foothills overshadowed by the Southern Alps. You can stand high above the city and dream of river gorges, mountain passes and the West Coast known for its tall stories, giant eels, rainforests and frequently quirky people derived from a melting pot of cultures that stormed to the goldfields during the 1860s.

But from the Port Hills you also look to the south, in the direction of Dunedin, Central Otago with its colourful Chinese goldfields heritage, Southland and Fiordland, and north, to the grape-growing regions of North Canterbury. Further north again are Kaikoura, the Marlborough Sounds and Nelson's famous Abel Tasman National Park where, every summer, posh Christchurch people agree to spend the summer clinking champagne glasses under wet, flapping canvas.

Every direction offers a part of this South Island journey, and every journey and destination is as different, and as exciting, as the next.

But, down in Harihari, George was perhaps lucky to get a sunny morning to work on his shop sign. South Westland is a region where rainfall is measured in metres rather than centimetres. Had Father Christmas's generosity and goodwill led him to George's chimney that Christmas he could well have arrived in the rain. In such circumstances, sooting his bright red tunic, he might have thought that George, too, was a miserable prick!

Setting out on a South Island journey.

Westward

CHAPTER 1

A HOME FOR THE SOUL

You feel the mist on your face and enjoy the honeyed smells of the beech forest. And if you look up you will see how the mountain mist, highlighting the crags and gullies, reveals the secrets of the bush.

Grace Adams

The truth is, had there been no Arthur's Pass I would probably not be here: I might have considered running away by the age of 10. Such was 1950s life in Christchurch. A dreary, sooty post-war town inhabited by strap-wielding schoolteachers, it offered little joy for any slightly sensitive kid. If Christchurch was hell then Arthur's Pass — a quaint alpine hamlet serving a national park and a trans-alpine railway — was heaven. It was as simple as that.

We spent happy family holidays in this tiny place dwarfed by mountains, and Arthur's Pass became the panacea for all ills. It is where I discovered that there is music in stillness, and magic in solitude. Arthur's Pass became the home for my soul and, I suspect, it still is.

The attraction was a wonderful alliance of railways, dramatic mountains topped by the beautifully sculptured low peak of Mount Rolleston, crystal-clear alpine streams, mysterious beech-forest tracks, idyllic cottages clad with brightly painted corrugated iron — and some delightfully eccentric people. Arthur's Pass had its origins in the 1860s when (Sir) Arthur Dudley Dobson found his route through the mountains, over the pass that bears his name and down through a treacherous cleft known as the Otira Gorge. A road of hairpin bends, plunging 400 metres in less than 8 kilometres, was subsequently cut from a precipice to pirate West Coast gold and bring it to Canterbury.

Over this road rumbled the famous Cobb & Co. horse-drawn coaches run by a legendary Irishman, Hugh Cassidy. Then, on 4 August 1923, the opening of the 5.3-mile (8554-metre) Otira railway tunnel was celebrated as one the great civil engineering feats of the British Empire. Indeed, it was the empire's longest tunnel, beating the Connaught Tunnel on the Canadian Pacific Railway by a quarter of a mile.

Brian Brake, New Zealand's most celebrated photographer, once lived at Arthur's Pass, as did ski pioneer Oscar Coberger, grandfather of New Zealand ski champion, Analise Coberger. But even more memorable for me was a mysterious Scotsman, Charlie Warden. Of course, to us children he was always Mr Warden. He arrived in Arthur's Pass in 1924 and settled into a corrugated iron hut he called Gaya. It was a former tunnelling engineer's dwelling for which he paid the princely sum of £24.

Mr. Warden, an old Scotsman and Arthur's Pass identity, who kept his mysteries.

Photography was one of his many interests. He had brought from Scotland a wonderful collection of handmade interlocking wood cameras and introduced Brian Brake to photography. Aged nine or 10, lost and grieving after the death of his mother, Brian Brake became fascinated by the magic of film processing in one of Gaya's darkened rooms.

My family, too, had a lot to do with this kindly Scottish bachelor whose heavily accented speech was filtered through an impressive nicotine-stained moustache. He was one of many people who bought the old tunnel workers' cottages for holiday houses, although in his case it was his only home.

Most early Arthur's Pass residents were not well off, so the dwellings were sold for about £20 — or less. And that was all they were worth, sited as they were in a gigantic rubbish dump created by the Otira Tunnel construction. Anything of no great value to the railway had been left behind, but the rubbish provided many useful items to repair and adapt the cottages. What the locals did not want nature, over time, kindly covered over.

Arthur's Pass began to look like a village and tourists started to arrive

Kb 968, a one-time stalwart of Arthur's Pass, steams through the mountains for the last time in June 1969.

when a lodge was built. Then, on 9 March 1929, the settlement was almost ruined, hit by an earthquake that caused tremendous damage to the town and the mountains. Many years later Mr Warden told us how he was on his way home from a dance when it struck. The railway tracks he was walking on twisted under his feet, water pipes in dwellings burst, chimneys came crashing down. Arriving home, most people were greeted by water and soot all over their carpets, and broken china, much of it given to them as wedding presents. Devastated people cleared out of Arthur's Pass but Charlie Warden stayed on. In 1930 he became the first resident ranger of the new Arthur's Pass National Park Board. His duties, which were to protect the flora and fauna, involved educating visitors arriving on train excursions and encouraging them not to take away alpine flowers — especially the spectacular *Ranunculus lyallii*, or mountain lily — by the armful.

The national park, largely the brainchild of botanist Dr Leonard Cockayne, subsequently became a botanists' paradise, attracting many curious specialists, including a curious Dr Hill from Kew Gardens in London.

Arthur's Pass was well established when I first arrived as a wide-eyed five-year-old. The railway with its huge, thundering Kb Class 4-8-4 steam locomotives was as impressive as the mountains. There was drama as west-bound and east-bound express trains met, and electric locomotives replaced steam for the long descent through the Otira Tunnel which started a short distance from the station. Daily railway antics provided entertainment for mothers with children. Fathers, more often than not, were mountain climbers. Some had been pioneer Canterbury mountaineers with several first ascents to their credit.

Away from the noisy railway my older brother and I were encouraged to discover the riches that are found only in nature. We were introduced to the awesome Devil's Punchbowl waterfall and, later, to the magical alpine world above the bushline. Arthur's Pass taught us values and a love for the natural world that would survive a lifetime. There was always a cottage we could rent cheaply for a family holiday. Indeed, many holidays were spent at Gaya.

But that was a long time ago. The world has moved on — and changed. Regrettably, the once idyllic township has been diminished by excessive road widening and an occasional disregard for compatible architecture. In November 1999 the road viaduct opened in the Otira

Gaya cottage, as it is remembered by the author.

Gorge. Undoubtedly a fine piece of modern engineering and completely compatible with its national park environment, it has nevertheless encouraged heavier traffic flows and even more speeding motorists. The Arthur's Pass I first discovered in the 1950s was a memorial to the Otira Tunnel builders. Perhaps it should have remained that way?

At every opportunity I still return, sometimes arriving on the Tranz-Alpine Express, promoted with some justification as one of the world's great scenic rail journeys. Away from the main road and, especially, above the bushline, Arthur's Pass is as beautiful and rewarding as ever. I have my special places where I will take friends who want to share a part of what is essentially myself. Arthur's Pass can still be a panacea for all ills.

Struggling to keep up with a sprightly 72-year-old, I am grateful when we pause at the highest point on the Devil's Punchbowl track. Low cloud descending on the mountains focuses our attention on the forest and the roaring white-water creek.

'You feel the mist on your face and enjoy the honeyed smells of the beech forest,' she tells me in a slightly high-pitched voice that belies her age. 'And if you look up you will see how the mountain mist, highlighting the crags and gullies, reveals the secrets of the bush.'

Grace Adams, my companion, is a 'guardian of Arthur's Pass'. She is also a long-time friend. 'I must be the worst grandmother in New Zealand,' she had once confided when I was visiting with my reporter's notepad. 'I'm always gadding around — tramping, skiing, rock-and-roll dancing and playing tennis. I'm a great believer in staying young. I see nothing unusual in wanting to climb a mountain ridge to see the sun rise. Skiing for me is just a magical experience. I'm not a top skier but I sure like going fast.'

She is also author of *Jack's Hut*, a compelling history and personal experience of growing up among the mountains, published in 1968. Her parents, Guy and Grace Butler, owned the hut, the one-time roadman's cottage that still stands near the summit of the pass. 'We would rent our New Brighton home for up to six weeks at a time and live at Jack's Hut. Arthur's Pass became my life. We didn't have a car and it was many years before I went anywhere else, or even knew what lay beyond Otira.'

She first thought of writing a book while jogging as fast as she could from Jack's Hut back to the Arthur's Pass settlement one day in 1961. As she ran her mind was also racing, 'like the wheels of a Cobb & Co. coach

Grace Adams studies a work depicting the Otira Gorge by her artist-mother Grace Butler.

churning up the dust of the past'. Grace has always had a love of words. She wanted to write about the coaching days in the Otira Gorge, building the railway tunnel, the old roadmen of Jack's Hut — Ned Roberts and Jack O'Kane — and, above all, her artist mother. As a teenager she started writing and reading radio scripts including the popular series, *Tales from the Southern Alps*. She had already climbed most of the Arthur's Pass mountains — Rolleston, Phipps and Murchison — but people also interested her, and the social events of an isolated 1940s alpine township.

'I used to ape my two elder sisters by pretending I was 16 when I was only 13. That was when we went to socials in the old railway refreshment rooms. There was an open fire and a ladies' department which was usually crammed with babies and prams. Mr Warden played the piano. I never saw him with music. If there was a modern piece he didn't know, we just hummed the tune and then he would play it.'

She would occasionally visit Mr Warden at his home. 'He had become very arthritic and would not have been able to get to his outside dunny in time during the night. So he had this large jerry pot, or "potty".' I called on him one morning about 11 a.m. with a message from my father. I knocked on the door and called out. Suddenly the door latch was free and the door could be pushed open. He was still in bed. He had opened the door from his bed, two rooms away from the front door, by yanking on a long string threaded through a series of pulleys.

'He welcomed me in and I sat down as he started another of his philosophical debates. But all the while my eyes furtively gazed at his potty, sitting on the cabinet beside his bed. It was full to the brim with yellow urine. On the top floated two apple cores.'

As a girl she met Brian Brake, whose father owned the Arthur's Pass store. Although he was almost the same age as Grace, Brian was a serious little boy with a shock of red curly hair and he seemed to be conceited. 'He was not the ordinary kind of child. By the time he was six years old he was acting like a little adult, especially when he was working behind the counter of his father's store. He also drove his father's truck. Blocks of wood had to be fastened to the pedals so he could reach them.'

Brian Brake and Grace Adams became lifelong friends. They corresponded during the 1960s and 1970s when Brian Brake was a renowned Magnum photographer living in Hong Kong. Before his death in 1988 he had plans for a photo essay of Arthur's Pass through the seasons as well as completing a new volume of *New Zealand: Gift of the Sea* with writer Maurice Shadbolt. Brian Brake had returned to

New Zealand to rediscover his home, having photographed the world's powerful people, and its poor. His work had been used in great international publications, including *National Geographic*. It had also been displayed in some of the world's most famous galleries in London, Paris and New York. His poignant photo essay depicting the monsoon in India is still widely exhibited.

'Even as a boy there was the mark of a real artist about him,' recalls Grace Adams. 'He never lost interest in Arthur's Pass. I believe Arthur's Pass was central to his love of beauty and nature. He always loved mountains, the snow and plant life — they all had a big effect on him. I am sure it was Arthur's Pass that eventually brought him back to New Zealand.

'Few people know that Brian Brake was also a promising pianist. He could have become a famous musician rather than a photographer. We both played the piano when we were at Arthur's Pass. I struggled, but Brian played with serenity and feeling. He could be electrifying when he touched the keys.'

These days the future of Jack's Hut is a little precarious although Grace does have a 1971 document in which the then Arthur's Pass National Park Board decreed to retain Jack's Hut as a historic place '... belonging to the park and the people of New Zealand as a link in the history of the country's early days'. Regrettably, its isolation also attracts a degree of vandalism.

Grace has her own 'hovel' down in the township. It is an old tunnel worker's cottage, now beautifully restored and fitted with a window sufficiently large to capture panoramic views of mountains and beech forest. It was Grace who introduced me to the idea of drinking the water from the Devil's Punchbowl, a spectacular, if drenching, experience as one cups ice-cold water just near where the spears of water crash 150 metres into the bowl at the base of the falls. The antic is best completed by getting 'a little wet on the inside' at the Chalet bar back in the township.

She is keen to write a biography about her parents and especially her mother's painting. Grace Butler, a landscape painter of the Canterbury School, was a plein-air artist with a special interest in capturing light and atmosphere in the Otira Gorge and among the alpine features of Arthur's Pass. Two of her teachers had been taught by Petrus van der Velden, Cecil Kelly and Sydney Thompson.

'I've been encouraged by well-known New Zealand artist Bill Sutton and art lecturer Julie King, but it's very hard to write about one's own mother. It's all the more difficult because she once said point blank, "Grace, you are never to write about me." She never allowed anything to be written about her because she said her paintings alone were sufficient.

'Sometimes I wonder why I get so stirred up. Who really cares if I write the biography or not. The world won't change much either way. I then have to tell myself that writing is all about telling the truth to yourself on paper.'

As a housewife with a family who never had the opportunity to go overseas, Grace Butler was an unusual professional painter. 'She was extremely talented. So little is known about her. She was a sweet little thing but she could become a tiger of a lady when something was really important.'

Grace Adams can recall a time when she thought no other place could possibly have the beauty of Arthur's Pass and Mount Rolleston. 'It will always be special but it is just one of the South Island's beautiful places. I have tramped in the Rees-Dart area which had once, like Arthur's Pass, also been a special place for my parents. They had lived at Paradise beyond the head of Lake Wakatipu for three months while my mother painted.'

Late in 1999 I met Haruko Morita who somehow, and irrevocably, stepped onto my Arthur's Pass patch. I had shown her a video of a Television New Zealand programme, *Inspiration*, made in 1987 when Brian Brake returned to New Zealand. She was captivated by the humility and talent of the photographer and, especially, his love for Arthur's Pass and its mountains. She wanted me to take her there and when she arrived she was not disappointed. She enjoyed experiencing the small town and particularly the interdenominational chapel with its view of the Avalanche Creek waterfall through plain-glass altar windows.

Haruko had graduated in philosophy from Hosei University in Tokyo — she told me she was fascinated by 'the way of thinking' — and subsequently spent a year living in Nagano, a mountainous part of Japan. She now thought trekking was all in her past, but she still loved the mountains. With another Japanese friend I took her to the Devil's Punchbowl waterfall for a hands-on experience with nature. Together we craned our necks to see the top of the falls, and then follow their progress to the base. All the while the patterns of water were changing into endless spectacular cascades — just a few metres away. And we were getting drenched. Haruko's short jet black hair was streaming water; her face was laughing with sheer delight.

In the car on the way home she quietly told me her story of the waterfall.

'It makes me feel good. It's the same feeling as good music. Musicians, artists, writers, and other people with talent also serve no practical purpose. They are just like water falling down. From top to bottom.

The Devil's Punchbowl is a striking feature close to Arthur's Pass township.

Endless. No one ever asks anyone to create anything beautiful. They cannot help doing it. We are always impressed by their creations as we are always impressed by the beautiful things of nature.'

On another occasion, down on the West Coast, we had stopped beside a lake to enjoy the evening colours. Haruko bent down to study a fern leaf. It had three parts in its basic design, there were three leaves to a branch and the entire structure could be separated into three parts. 'The design is also endless, like the waterfall,' she told me. 'It is also like the circular mandala design, a symbol of Buddhism. For me, the mandala represents the one universe with lots of Buddhist gods inside. It is endless, like birth and death. It is all continuing, like nature. When I see this fern in New Zealand I can so easily imagine the mandala picture.'

And at Arthur's Pass we climbed Avalanche Peak. I knew Haruko could do it despite her considerable doubts. With the weather threatening to deteriorate we climbed the Avalanche Creek track, starting near the chapel. Above the bushline, in a patch of almost black cloud, we felt the cold seep through our jackets, and for a time views below and above were lost in the murk. Eventually, with the temperature becoming more bearable, we climbed into a lighter cloud. Then we broke free. Etched against a blue sky, our alpine peak towered a short distance above. Clouds scudded past just below its summit.

We spent the best part of two hours sitting on the summit, often in silence. The clouds continually changed; descending to hide the mountains in a whiteout, then lifting, streaming away from ridges to reveal the shape of the peaks. Mount Rolleston and its Crow ice glacier were spectacular. We descended the narrow summit ridge and, like a couple of delirious school kids, ran down parts of the mountain, often colliding and collapsing, laughing, in a patch of late-spring snow, until we reached the bush line at the top of Scotts Track. Near the bottom of the mountain we stopped, standing on a rock outcrop just off the track. It has always been one of my special spots, giving a view of the village in one direction, and in another, the full length of the Devil's Punchbowl waterfall, seemingly distant across the narrow valley. Light drizzle settled on Haruko's smooth cheeks. Soon she led the way down the track, turning to me with a smile to say, 'Roy san, I think we need to drink some beer.'

Haruko returned to Japan, but a part of her will always remain among my cherished memories of Arthur's Pass, as will old Mr Warden. He once showed me a map marking where he wanted to be buried, near the track to the Devil's Punchbowl. Regrettably, that was not to be, and his unpretentious gravestone is found in All Saints churchyard in the Christchurch suburb of Burwood. The simple inscription reads 'Charles Warden late of Arthur's Pass'. He had lived among mountains, yet he was not a mountain person in any real sense. He always wore sandshoes and he always moved slowly; his level of exertion would never have made him puff too much.

Charles Edward Warden was born in Edinburgh on 2 February 1879, the son of Francis Warden, a draper's bookkeeper, and Jessica Warden. He sailed for New Zealand on 21 November 1902 aboard RMS *Corinthic*; his name is listed among the second saloon passengers. For some years he lived in Christchurch, at 86 Salisbury Street, where he was a builder but apparently not as successful as he might have wished. He became a close friend of the eccentric and radical Professor Alexander Bickerton whose notable pupil, Ernest Rutherford, was to become the father of nuclear physics. Charlie Warden also painted a pretty fair watercolour of the professor's Wainoni house.

He died on 16 May 1959, having spent several years in Burwood Hospital, and I was one of the pallbearers at his funeral, along with my father and brother. I recall the wonderful family holidays spent in Gaya during the years he was in hospital. The cosy cottage was just as he had left it: books piled high, the jerry pot still under his bed, and the wind-up gramophone with its collection of 1950s 78s. It was a home jammed full of treasures.

But for the rest of the time I would get my 'Arthur's Pass fix' by cycling about 10 kilometres on a Sunday afternoon to Burwood Hospital and sitting beside Mr Warden's bed. He was a philosopher as well as a nature lover. I was still very young, barely a teenager, so much of what he said went over my head. I just enjoyed listening to his deep Scottish burr, still being filtered through that generous moustache. I suspect this is where my own love for stories and storytelling began.

Yet his life remains an enigma. What was his background? Why did he come to live, alone, in such an isolated part of the world? Was it simply, as I have always suspected, a sad story of lost love?

CHAPTER 2

ON YOUR BIKE

I once wanted a bicycle so badly, I went out and stole one.
                                    Fiona Shaffrey

The day began as intended. Old man nor-wester was still hiding high up in the mountains as the first few kilometres were demolished from a 70-kilometre ride across the Canterbury Plains to Springfield. It was supposed to be a bit of a warm-up for a leisurely three-day trans-alpine bike ride, but by late morning the gale had been unleashed. State Highway 73, I was fast discovering, is aimed at that wind. The Cateye cycle computer was registering 11 kilometres an hour, then it dropped to a miserable 8. Each kilometre took an amazingly long time to tick over. Untrained muscles began to scream.

When I was a 1950s schoolboy, travelling agog aboard the West Coast Express to spend holidays at Arthur's Pass, I was immersed in dreams. One was to drive a steam locomotive to the pass. Another — only if the first could not be fulfilled — was to do the trip by bike. Regrettably, a cherished ambition to become a locomotive driver had little encouragement from those I was obliged to share my early life with, my parents in particular. In any event, by the time my school days were over, the last great steam locomotives were chuffing confidently towards the scrap heap or transport museums.

The best part of half a century passed before the alternative dream was fulfilled. By then, I was middle-aged, and my horizons had been extended. My teenage daughter Kirsten, showing no signs of mastering the skills required for a car driver's licence, had flown me across the South Island in a small aircraft. Could the coast-to-coast pedalling adventure be a sort of misguided encore? I planned to follow as closely as possible the rail route of the famous TranzAlpine.

One sunny Sunday December morning I set off. My bike was a

Raleigh, the same brand as I once rode to school, but this one was a 1990s mountain version with 21-speed Shimano gears. It had been serviced and fitted with slick road tyres, and a pair of spanking new pannier bags.

Plugged into my Walkman, I heard an interesting Concert FM discussion about how mid-twentieth-century music began to reflect the spiritual nature of mankind. It was a breakthrough — no longer were

Making friends down near Lake Poerua, west of the Alps.

we merely a regrettable assemblage of mechanical muscle and bone. Obviously, the scriptwriter had never pedalled a bike into a Canterbury nor-wester. My threatening-to-fail knee joints were warning me of a need to be more adept mechanically than spiritually. And I was having to get used to the shocking disregard for cyclists displayed by too many truck drivers whose big rigs passed so close that there was a real danger of being mangled under unfriendly wheels.

For all that, I was enjoying a rare freedom. Somehow, I was being enveloped by the environment and I reached Kirwee in just over two hours. Relaxing on the crisp grass under trees, I called my son on my mobile. From, I suspect, an exclusive Auckland café, he casually asked how long it had taken to cover the 40 kilometres. I told him. He said it was pathetic. 'You could have done it in 20 minutes, even in your old car,' he told me. In defence I feebly mentioned his speeding fines.

Springfield, at the western edge to the Canterbury Plains, took just over five hours' riding time, much longer than planned. But I arrived at Smylie's YHA in good spirits. My host, John Keiko, led me upstairs to a beautifully furnished attic room in one of Springfield's old colonial cottages. Backpackers, it seemed, could enjoy splendid comforts at bargain basement prices.

Down in the local pub another backpacker, Bas, from the Netherlands, was drinking beer against the background of a large Speights Coast-to-Coast poster. This annual triathlon event takes most competitors coast-to-coast, west to east, in one day. I was taking three days to go east to west.

'When I'm quite old I would love to be living in New Zealand,' Bas said with a grin. When I asked his age and what he considered would be 'quite old', he answered 47 to the first question and about 55 to the second. Regrettably, I already qualified for his 'quite old' category.

Springfield is the birthplace of Rewi Alley, the illustrious Kiwi who spent almost a lifetime working in China. Although my mother had always talked to me about him, I grew up knowing little about this remarkable man.

From my attic window I could see Springfield's striking monument and information kiosk commemorating Alley's life, so I went to investigate.

This twentieth-century champion of internationalism had set out during the 1920s to discover a seemingly doubtful case for a relationship between China and tiny New Zealand. In 1927 he was working as a fire

Rewi Alley and friends in China. (Photograph courtesy Bill Willmott)

inspector and factory inspector in Shanghai. Travelling widely, he became involved in a number of humanitarian projects, forming co-operatives that enabled people to work together to produce essentials. He was headmaster of a school he established for peasant children, a writer and poet, a peace campaigner. He worked with the Chinese during times of great poverty, the Japanese invasion, revolutions and when the Communists came to power. He met and won the respect of Chairman Mao and, in 1961, attended a conference against atomic and hydrogen bombs in Japan.

Accused by some New Zealand politicians as having Communist sympathies, he nevertheless represented his native country as unofficial ambassador for the New Zealand Peace Council. In 1971 he was awarded an honorary Doctorate of Literature by the Victoria University of Wellington. In 1981 he was made an honorary citizen of Beijing and, in 1985, of Gansu Province. The same year he was awarded the Queen's Service Order by the New Zealand government. He died, aged 90, in 1987. His ashes are scattered in Gansu, near Shandan.

Born a South Islander and named after a famous North Island Maori chief, he had helped three quarters of the world's population understand the other quarter — China. But still I wondered why my mother had always talked to me, especially, about Rewi Alley. I was about to go and prepare for the next day's ride when my eye caught a familiar date. Rewi was born on 2 December. We shared the same birthday.

Springfield was a one-time staging post on the railway between Christchurch and the West Coast. Here, six magnificent Kb class 4-8-4 steam locomotives were stabled for the 69-kilometre mountain run through to Arthur's Pass. These days Springfield marks the TranzAlpine's entry into the mountains. Although I have made the trip on many occasions, I never tire of the smug feeling as I sit in a carriage listening to the oohs and aahs of appreciative international rail travellers while the TranzAlpine snakes above the Waimakariri Gorge, passing through 16 tunnels and crossing dizzying steel viaducts. But my bike was to take a different route, tackling Porters Pass, at 944 metres the highest point on the trans-alpine State Highway 73.

Rain was threatening as I set off at about 9 a.m. for the 84-kilometre ride to Arthur's Pass. John Keiko had suggested I could wait and catch the coast-to-coast bus. 'The bus also carries bikes,' he offered — but motorised transport was not an option.

Lake Pearson captures the eye along the trans-alpine trail between Springfield and Arthur's Pass.

The wind had dropped and the Raleigh was soon clocking a refreshing 20 kilometres an hour or more. Fourteen easy kilometres later I rested, and then set out on the steep climb to Porters Pass. The uphill struggle, over about 3 kilometres, was less gruelling than I anticipated. One of the dreaded obstacles of the ride had been surmounted. What followed was a series of rolling downhill stretches with the rain stinging against my unprotected face. But the road soon climbed once more, levelling out on the long straight past Castle Hill, so named because of an unexpected outcrop of striking limestone tors set a short distance back from the highway.

Writer and explorer Samuel Butler strayed this way on horseback sometime during the 1860s. I suspect he saw the limestone shapes through a strange light and considered them grotesque. They feature, albeit relocated, in his classic novel *Erewhon*. But for me, Preisner's 'Requiem for My Friend', and the soprano, Elzbieta Towarnicka, provided the perfect accompaniment on my Walkman as I cruised beside this highlight of the western road.

Had the day been pleasant, the afternoon ride beside Lake Pearson and the upper Waimakariri, and into the Bealey Valley, would have been a delight. Instead, rain gradually saturated my inner clothing, and I was constantly being made aware of the unnecessary dangers of touring cycling in New Zealand. Near Cass, a milk tanker and trailer overtaking a line of cars showed no inclination to revert to his legal left-hand lane. Luckily, before the dare-devil truckie with seemingly murderous intent completely filled my vision, I was able to ride off the road and cool down in comparative safety.

The slow pace of life on a bike did offer its compensations, allowing time to look into streams as I rode across numerous bridges, and watch snow clouds close in on the mountains. Almost asleep on my wheels, I rode into Arthur's Pass at 4.20 p.m. Life was restored by a sudden blast from a hooter that almost had me falling off my bike. Not another bloody truckie? The culprit this time was the eastbound TranzAlpine emerging from the Otira Tunnel. My arrival at Arthur's Pass had been perfectly timed. That night it snowed to low levels on the mountains.

Snug in my bunk at the Sir Arthur Dudley Dobson Youth Hostel I dreamed happily of my childhood days at the pass. I thought of the keas and their comical gait as they pranced on a mountain summit, always looking for mischief, and their skilful flight, revealing flashes of bright orange under their wings. I could almost hear their cry, 'kea, kea,

Veteran locomotive driver Bill Frazer recalled the trans-alpine coaching days in verse.

kea . . .' I was awake with a start. It was 5 a.m. The squawking keas were outside my window. My bike! Visions of tyres torn to shreds were unfounded as the delinquent keas hastily departed marginally ahead of a shower of surprisingly well-aimed rocks.

Next morning's ride was to start with an uninviting stiff climb to the summit of Arthur's Pass (914 metres) and down the infamous Otira Gorge. The latter had been improved by the recently opened Otira Viaduct, a stylish example of modern engineering that eliminates the notoriously steep zigzag section. It was cold as I stopped briefly to photograph my bike at Jack's Hut, and then continued to the top of the pass. I had wanted to see the beautiful *Ranunculus Lyallii* in bloom, but flowering had been early. Disappointed, I was greeted with a few rain-wrecked petals.

The descent of the gorge was frightening. As I released the brakes on the smooth surface of the new viaduct the Cateye was showing 40 kilometres an hour within seconds. And stopping on those steep grades took an alarming lapse of time.

I spared a thought for a time when Cobb & Co. and five-horse teams were the kings of the Otira road and for an acquaintance, Bill Frazer, a one-time New Zealand Railways electric locomotive driver working on the Otira to Arthur's Pass section. At the age of 96 he had recited from memory the haunting 'Ballad of Otira Gorge'. Bill had told me he heard the ballad while yarning in Mrs Penhallurick's Hotel with Tremayne Curnow, vicar of Malvern and father of New Zealand poet Allen Curnow. During the 1920s the Otira Tunnel workings were included in the Malvern parish and the Reverend Mr Curnow, also a talented writer of light verse, enjoyed the company of the tunnel workers and the railwaymen, often spending the night in Otira. But the Cobb & Co. coach trip down the Otira Gorge, frequently in deplorable weather, belonged to the realm of nightmares.

> The view it fairly scares me stiff
> The road's a ledge along a cliff
> The wheels go near it, heavens if
> They made a deviation.
> I only hope that I survive
> This perfect nightmare of a drive
> To offer thanks when I arrive
> Safe at Otira Station.

Cobb & Co. plied the road between Christchurch and Hokitika from 1866. As the railway advanced inland from either coast, the coach journey became shorter. Rails from the West Coast reached Otira in 1900, and by 1914 trains were also steaming up to Arthur's Pass. For the next nine years Cobb & Co., New Zealand's last scheduled horse-drawn coach service, joined the railheads while work was completed on the long tunnel beneath the Southern Alps. Even then, the Otira Gorge was becoming renowned for its spectacular scenery, especially in late summer when the native rata splashed scarlet among the sombre green bush.

Most frustrating were two years of unpleasant journeying over the hill after the tunnelling had been completed in 1921. (It took that long to equip the tunnel with overhead gear for the electric locomotives.) Sitting on the topmost seat ('ladies and baggage go inside') the Reverend Mr Curnow continued to pencil his lines as his clergyman's collar formed a perfect funnel to catch the inevitable rain:

I'm no seeker after thrills
I'd rather travel under hills
Than over them with rain and chills
In constant trepidation
I only hope some other day
To travel back the tunnel way
So may no further hitch delay
That blessed perforation.

The Reverend Mr Curnow did travel back the tunnel way. A letter from Allen Curnow confirmed that his father had been delighted to receive the government invitation card for the Otira Tunnel opening ceremony on 4 August 1923. He returned home clutching a piece of blue ribbon cut at the special event.

Almost frozen I, too, was no seeker after thrills as my laden two wheels negotiated the final steep grades of the gorge. At last I could relax and cruise down more gentle slopes to stop at the first of many traditional

A preserved Cobb & Co. 'The Burton' recalls brave days of trans-alpine journeys in the Canterbury Museum. It was built by A.G. Howland of Christchurch.

West Coast pubs. There I discovered, arguably, one of the world's worst meat pies, mixed poorly with a cup of lukewarm coffee.

But the West Coast is undoubtedly a cyclist's paradise. For the first time my Raleigh was running freely on the almost continuous gentle downgrade to the Tasman Sea. This third day was the longest (103 kilometres) but also the easiest. Soon the sun was starting to warm me through. Then, another truckie was rushing down the road behind me and I was riding against a steep embankment offering no escape. But this time I heard him expertly working down through endless gears as he approached, ready to slow his big rig behind me if he could not pass safely on the narrow winding road. This was something the less-than-charitable Canterbury truckies were not prepared to do for a cyclist.

If there was a real sense of achievement on the ride, it was on this section from Otira to Jackson. I was through the mountains and the Cateye kilometres were amassing at a much quicker pace. I imagined I was riding beside the old West Coast Express as I knew it in the 1950s. Running down the Otira River beside me and into the Taramakau River Valley, it was trailing a plume of white smoke. The wheels were spinning and the piston rods flashing as, like me, the express was enjoying a new freedom, having endured the trans-alpine crossing. And West Coast hospitality was to the fore. Without fail truckies waved and tooted, as did Tranz Rail drivers.

Lunch was washed down with a generous glass of beer at Jackson's pub, supposedly famous for possum pies — although on this occasion these were conspicuously absent from the menu. A short distance down the road, I took the sharp right-hand turn and crossed the long Taramakau River to follow the TranzAlpine rail route to Moana and Greymouth. As I rode though a sparsely populated rural landscape, scattered intermittently with hideaway houses, I recalled those who had contributed to the special character of the Coast.

I passed Inchbonnie, once home to Jim and Fiona Shaffrey. Jim, who had been born a Coaster and became a farmer, had the maddening ability to unfailingly look bright-eyed in the morning, despite being rendered virtually incapable just a few short hours before, after sharing a bottle of whisky.

Fiona had grown up in Waimate. In 1942 she became the new sole-charge teacher at Inchbonnie school and she was still delightfully very much the schoolmistress when I met her in 1993. Then in her 70s, she was occasionally relief teaching up at Otira.

She had once been the school bus driver. When asked about this she replied, perhaps a little defensively, 'I once rolled the school bus.' That was in 1974, when Fiona Shaffrey was then one of two teachers at Rotomanu School, and she took over the school bus from Jack Fitzsimmons. 'I was dodging this big black cow that came charging out when I was going downhill on a shingle road. It had just been graded. I just thought I would go off onto the grass verge. But a hump was hidden in the long grass. And the bus, a little red and yellow 12-seater, rolled over gently onto its roof.

'Petrol was pouring down the windscreen, too close to the hot motor. So I turned off the key, grabbed the fire extinguisher and sprayed it around. That was the only thing that upset the kids. They had been as good as gold till then. But they started screaming blue murder once they saw the foam. So I kicked open the doors and we got out. Then a precious little ugly daughter shook herself and said, "I'm having it for news."

'No one was hurt, except I've had a cranky neck ever since. Instead

Fiona Shaffrey remembers railway days and a mishap with the school bus.

of a blast from the Education Board, I got a lot of commendations. The other teacher had phoned the board and said I was badly hurt, but the first thing I did was to think of the children and spray the bus with foam. There might have been some negligence. I might have been going a wee bit fast down the hill. And I didn't want to jam on the brakes. Nobody had told the traffic cop. He came up to the school quite concerned because I had never reported the accident. He was the school traffic officer as well!'

Not long before my trans-alpine bike ride Jim Shaffrey had died, and Fiona had gone to live down in Greymouth. Had she still been in Inchbonnie I know she would have wanted to see my mountain bike. A devout Roman Catholic, she had burst into laughter when she confessed she had once wanted a bicycle so badly that she had stolen one!

Old Jack Fitzsimmons, who had previously driven the school bus, had arrived on the Coast during the 1940s as a lamb buyer for Borthwicks. Subsequently, he was involved in sawmilling and farming. A big man, his claim to fame was being the proud great-nephew of Bob Fitzsimmons, a turn-of-the-century boxing champion, and one of the greatest ring fighters of all time, with three world titles.

Bob Fitzsimmons was not a Coaster. Born in Cornwall, he arrived in New Zealand in 1871 as a nine-year-old with his pioneering parents. He grew up in Timaru where his massive strength was developed working as a blacksmith. Against his parents' wishes he took up boxing at the age of 15, and eventually arrived in the United States. He was never taken seriously. Already almost bald, apart from a tuft of reddish hair drooping over each ear, he had pathetically skinny arms and legs, and his freckled figure was dismissed as that of 'a physical freak' rather than a boxer. His huge strength lay in his broad shoulders, heavily muscled back and huge hands.

In 1891, in New Orleans, Fitzsimmons knocked out the world middleweight champion Jack Dempsey in the thirteenth round and took over the title. Then in 1897 he took the world heavyweight title from James J. Corbett at Carson City, Nevada, with the famous Fitzsimmons 'solar plexus punch'. Finally, in 1903, aged 41, he took the newly constituted light-heavyweight title from George Gardner at San Francisco. Fitzsimmons was still boxing when he was 51. He died in the United States on 23 October 1917. For all his fame, his name is surprisingly absent from lists of New Zealand twentieth-century sporting greats.

These days the only Fitzsimmons on the Coast is Jack's son, Murray. 'Dad was always proud of his family connection with the world boxing champion. They wanted him to box too, but he never did.' Jack Fitzsimmons died in 1970.

Murray is a Coast-born Fitzsimmons, and the only member of the family left at Inchbonnie. 'I have a sister, but she lives in Hong Kong,' he said. 'They also wanted me to take up boxing because I'm supposed to look a bit like Bob Fitzsimmons. I went bald, too, when I was about 21. Yes, I'm also proud to be related to one of the world's greatest ring fighters, but boxing wasn't for me.'

Of a more gentle nature was Rene Morgan who spent many years at Mitchell's hotel on the southern shores of Lake Brunner. When I saw her she was 96 and quick-witted, and living on her own in Christchurch just before Christmas 1998. Her daughter was visiting from Wellington and the two were looking forward to enjoying a picnic Christmas dinner beside Lake Pearson.

Rene, a refined young woman from Liverpool, married Ted Morgan, a West Coaster and marine engineer who had sailed on some of the

Christchurch-bound express about to travel through the Otira Tunnel to Arthur's Pass in 1963.

world's famous liners. They took over Mitchell's in 1923. Beer in a 10-gallon keg was brought in from Kumara, 14 miles away, on a horse-drawn cart. Later, the keg was tied to the running board of the Morgans' first car. Rene said she struggled to get used to the big New Zealanders who worked in 'the bush', and she had never heard so much swearing!

She delighted in telling the story of her first experience in the bar. She was alone when her first customer asked, 'Got a square rigger?' Rene answered, 'Oh no, we've only got a launch!'

'The man just asked me "Where's Ted?" and I directed him to the woolshed. Soon I saw the two of them with big smiles. I thought he was asking about a sailing yacht, but I was informed that a "square rigger" was a square gin bottle. Its square shape held a little more than a round bottle. I never lived that incident down. The story got around and was told in Greymouth hotels for years.'

Further down the valley I was cycling across streams with names that delightfully reflected early European journeying: Mosquito Creek, Puzzle Creek, Crooked River and Tube Creek. I am sure, too, that a Dead Man's Creek may have passed beneath my wheels. And then, at the top of a steep rise, I was overlooking the expanse of Lake Brunner and Moana. Beyond the Arnold River I could see regenerated rainforest.

These days about 80 per cent of indigenous West Coast forest is under conservation order. The idea is for sawmilling to progress from unsustainable to sustainable forest management, but for all that, logging and conservation on the West Coast remains a subject fraught with controversy. Some old timber men lived to express regret for the plunder of South Island forests. Others mellowed, with a passion for trees.

A.J. (Alex) Brownlee's family started felling timber at Pelorus in Marlborough in the 1860s, and finally closed down their Lake Brunner mill several years ago. In 1891 the Brownlees imported New Zealand's first bush steam lokey, a Chapman with a vertical steam boiler. It went to work on wooden rails (until they collapsed) through the Kaituna Valley in the Marlborough Sounds. Alex Brownlee, a profoundly gruff character with a good-natured sense of humour, was 88 when I caught up with him in Christchurch some years ago. He went to Bell Hill near Moana in 1925, just two years after the first load of Brownlee & Co. timber was railed to Canterbury through the new Otira Tunnel. He was employed in the sawmill's workshop maintaining the lokeys and other steam-driven gear.

Retired forester Alex Brownlee, a gruff character with a sense of humour.

'Bell Hill was as isolated as blazes. We must have had 50 miles of bush tramway on the West Coast,' he recalled. 'Everything went by tram. The only way to get the 10 miles from Bell Hill to Ruru, where a sawmill stood beside the main West Coast railway, was on the tram.

'We would take the lokey and a coal bin whenever the boys went to play football at Te Kinga on a Sunday. We played league, not rugby, because we all worked on Saturday. No one played rugby on a Sunday. Of course, there was a pub at Te Kinga. We would put the wobbly ones in the coal bin for the ride home.

'If someone was missing next morning we would have a look over the side of the coal bin and he would still be there. We also played football at Nelson Creek, about 12 miles out from Bell Hill. Bull Williams, one of Nelson Creek's two butchers, never locked his door. After the game we would go in and whack off a few sausages and take them to the pub, and cook them on a shovel over the fire. Bull knew what was going on.'

Runaways and crashes on the tramways became a part of everyday life. Towards the end of the tramway in the 1960s a loaded train got away on the long grade down to Ruru. Alex's son Ross was driving when the lokey jumped the points and careered on towards the mill, whistling as it went to warn everyone before it crossed the main road. The loaded logs took another track — towards the workshop where Alex was working on a boat. 'The doors were closed because I didn't want everyone to know what I was doing. Next thing two bloody great truck loads of logs crashed through the doors. That was the end of the boat. It was crushed to pieces. Moments earlier, I'd been working in the damned thing.'

Bringing kegs of beer down from Moana to the start of the tramway at Ruru, about 3 kilometres along the main line, was another experience. The keg fitted nicely on the NZR rails and could be rolled. 'Ye Gods, what we would do just for a few beers. Those days [the 1920s] the beer was all hops, and by the time we got a keg to Bell Hill it was all froth when we turned on the tap. We called it "fighting beer".'

But Alex said most people got the wrong impression about drinking on the Coast. It was mostly social drinking, and when it came to boozing the Coasters could not hold a candle to the Canterbury crowd. 'There were Chinese — survivors from the gold-rush days — living near Nelson Creek. They were about the only people who could grow vegetables on the Coast. They used to bring vegetables to town on poles balanced over their shoulders. They sold vegetables all round the town and finished up in the pub. The Chinese were great on the whisky. "Clanky water" they called it.'

Hundreds of kilometres of bush tramway have returned to nature or become walkways. Modern forestry is mostly worked by helicopters. At Bell Hill gold mining was now causing more destruction than any former sawmill, Alex claimed. He rarely saw the land clear-felled, and today much of the forest is regenerating, although he admits it takes 60 years or so for a rimu to mature. 'Many people on the Canterbury side of the mountains have never seen a rimu.' He still owned a private reserve of native timber in the Marlborough Sounds, and strongly disagreed with a government three-year moratorium during the early 1990s for the felling of native timber on private land. 'That was a big mistake. It was an opportunity for people to knock down many magnificent big trees that sawmillers had previously decided to leave standing. It was a damn shame.'

Pedalling the last three hours from Moana to Greymouth in balmy afternoon sunshine was sheer pleasure, despite one knee telling me 'no more hills'. I paused at the top of a rise to call Claire Lhermitte, the manager of Greymouth's Kainga-Ra YHA, confirming my booking, and to say I would easily get there before the 10 p.m. closing time. At 3 o'clock in the afternoon she was mystified by my call. 'Why Roy,' she said, 'you could walk to Greymouth in that time.'

I replied, 'Well actually I'm on a bike, pedalling!'

I had long given up listening to my Walkman, preferring the sounds of the countryside you cannot hear from a motor vehicle. And the temperature became warmer and warmer. The last few kilometres beside the Grey River was into a stiff head wind coming off the pounding Tasman Sea. It was not cold like the prevailing 'Barber' that funnels downstream from the mountains, so sharp, the locals will tell you, that 'it'll cut your bloody throat.'

If anything, my trans-alpine ride ended in anti-climax — as indeed it does for the TranzAlpine rail journey. Arriving at the YHA, it was as if I was merely repeating a well-worn habit; this is how everyone arrives home at the end of a perfect day, on a bike.

CHAPTER 3

HARD-CASE HOTEL

*We're popular with backpacker travellers
and curious yuppies.*
Linda Osborn

In May 1995, while I was returning to Christchurch from Greymouth, curiosity about two defiant women took me on a detour off the main drag for my first visit to Blackball.

A year had passed since Blackball's historic two-storey hotel in Hart Street had been renamed Formerly The Blackball Hilton and so far there had been no protest. A previous owner of what had been the Blackball Hilton was taken to task by the multinational hotel chain for daring to use the brandname. For 20 years the name had stuck — until Blackball was confronted by the unquestioned might of the hoteliers. The Blackball Hilton (then a backpackers' hostel) was subsequently sold in March 1994 to Jane Wells and Linda Osborn, on the understanding that their establishment had no name.

In reinstating the Hilton name and merely adding the word 'formerly' the two women seemed hellbent on preserving Blackball's devil-may-care past that inspired such radicals as 'Fighting' Bob Semple and Paddy Webb — both of whom had leading roles in early Labour governments — Pat Hickey, William Balderstone and other colourful characters.

At first glance Blackball, a small, almost forgotten one-time coal-mining town 12 kilometres to one side of the highway from Stillwater to Greymouth, shows few scars from a militancy that shaped New Zealand labour protest from 1908 through to the infamous miners' strike of 1931. Blackball's position in a sleepy hollow overlooked by the Paparoa Ranges, locals will tell you, is a deception. The little settlement is still capable of hitting the national headlines, even for the sake of a hotel name.

Jane Wells arrived in Blackball sometime in the 1980s, having taught tourism and communications at Greymouth's Tai Poutini Polytechnic. She was the Blackball grocer until she married the butcher Pat Kennedy, known worldwide for his famed Blackball Salami Company. Linda Osborn, an aspiring saxophone player, previously worked for the West Coast Regional Council. She was attracted to Blackball a little earlier than Jane, claiming the title of 'alternative lifestyler'.

Within six months of buying the hotel the two women had upgraded the building and old bar to a stage where the licence was reissued. For the first time in 30 years beer was pulled once again in August 1994, and glasses placed on the same distinctive curved bar counter that has remained intact, if unused, since 1968. But drinkers could no longer enjoy a smoke with their beer: the hotel became the first totally smoke-free building on the West Coast.

'We're popular with backpacker travellers and curious yuppies,' said Linda. 'Most guests are Kiwis with some folk from overseas, mainly from Europe. One German traveller has been here on four occasions looking for a genuine New Zealand town that has resisted becoming the flashy tourist resort. We also reopened the hotel, especially the bar and dining facilities, to local people. We even have an EFTPOS. Blackball people no longer need to go to Greymouth for their pensions.'

Soon after their purchase, the pair had to think about a new name.

Linda Osborn, left, and Jane Wells defy an international hotel chain at Formerly The Blackball Hilton.

They spent a month sifting through a raft of suggestions. 'Hilt Inn' was a popular starter but 'Formerly The Blackball Hilton' did have a suitably radical ring about it. 'The new name was a very smart move by Linda and Jane,' I was later told by a previous owner who had been embroiled in the Hilton affair. Blackball had acquiesced to international might but the rechristening had saved face. And no wonder, when the hotel stands as a monument to the town's militant past.

In 1908, two years before the hotel was built, Semple, Webb and Hickey joined forces in Blackball to help fellow coal miners win their case over extending crib (lunch) time from 15 to 30 minutes. Hickey was the first to walk off the job and the ensuing strike ended a 12-year period when New Zealand was known internationally for its strike-free workplaces. A mainly successful outcome resulted in the formation of the Miners' Federation, led by the 'Red Feds' and later the Federation of Labour.

Then, from 1925 to 1928, Blackball was the New Zealand Communist Party headquarters and those years were said to have been the party's strongest. Blackball Communists were influenced by Yorkshire-born William Balderstone who had learned his radical ways in British Columbia. His equally militant wife, Annie, is said to have taught a socialist creed in Sunday school.

Such is the history recalled at Formerly The Blackball Hilton where works by local artists and relics from the two best-known miners' strikes are displayed in the hotel's 'First on the Left' gallery and TV room. And gracing one entire wall are the 1931 strikers' red flags inscribed 'No Scab Labour' and 'United We Stand'. On another wall much of Blackball's history can be read on old newspapers pasted there by previous owners. One story is headlined, 'If you don't like the meals, cook your own'. According to Jane, 'You still can!'

Jane soon became established as local historian as well as barmaid. She can tell about a time when 30 or so police commandeered the hotel from 15 June 1931 to keep law and order in the town. The miners' strike over shocking working conditions — caused mainly through absentee overseas mine owners and an effort by managers to halve the workforce — continued for about six months. Balderstone then defied the union to establish the Blackball Creek Coal Company, intending to work part of the mine by tribute.

Union members' bitterness was increased when they realised Balderstone had ratted while still receiving strike pay. His claim to 'uphold the best traditions of trade unionism' and employ only Blackball unionists did not wash; the miners wasted no time in declaring the Blackball Creek Coal Company black. But by September 1931 the employers considered they had won the battle (even though the mine closed); the depression years were to follow, the union was in tatters, and radical Blackball was seemingly out of steam. The coal mine was taken over by the government in 1940 and worked until it closed on 25 September 1964. Many of the town's 1200 inhabitants left. Blackball's future was in doubt.

The dwindling population was a factor in the hotel (then known as the Dominion) losing its liquor licence. In 1968 Westland Breweries sold the building to the Canterbury Mineral and Lapidary Club for the princely sum of $551.50. The club chose the hotel as a suitable base for West Coast fossicking but was forced to sell within a few years when the building failed to meet fire regulations.

The hotel was bought and upgraded by Mike Graham who was the first to use the Blackball Hilton name. (An alternative was 'Club Med Blackball'.) You might suspect it was a facetious attempt to upstage an esteemed international hotel chain but one Historic Places source claims

These days a backpackers' hostel, Formerly The Blackball Hilton, opened in 1910, stands as a memorial to a radical past.

Inside, newspapers pasted to walls recall the hotel's and Blackball's history.

Hilton to be the name of a one-time Blackball mine manager. There is a Hilton Street in town.

The story of the Hilton debacle has already become part of West Coast folklore and continues to be retold with embellishment at the hotel bar. It all happened when another previous owner, who does not wish to be named, saw a similar backpackers' hostel in Queenstown also calling itself the Hilton. He phoned the hostel and complained, only to be told to get lost. He admitted to the Queenstown proprietor that, had their roles been reversed, he would probably have made a similar remark. But he said that, with Queenstown's high profile, it would not be long before someone noticed.

Lo and behold, someone from London, whose job was to sort out people using the Hilton name, arrived in Queenstown. The proprietor agreed to drop the name (rumour has it that the matter was settled with a sum of money from the genuine Hilton), but our man from London was told about another outfit, in Blackball, also called Hilton.

The Hilton representative did not visit Blackball, preferring to work through a Wellington lawyer. The then proprietor could have dug in his toes but the Hilton people could have crushed any opposition — it would have been like using a hammer to squash a fly. 'It might have been worth a fight had our Hilton name been in use for 50 years. But it wasn't worth it for a mere 20 years. As it was, I thought the whole thing was handled quite well by the genuine Hilton people. 'It wasn't an unhappy experience for us. We got on television and actually got a lot of great publicity for Blackball. Blackball is an amazing little town with deep political roots that captures the imagination of an incredible number of people. Peter Tapsell, later to become Speaker of the House, stayed with us on at least six occasions. The Warratahs have stayed. They all enjoyed the experience.'

Jane and Linda were still at Blackball as the new millennium dawned, although they had put their hotel up for sale. 'We have certainly had no trouble with our new name,' Jane said, 'although an American once stopped here for afternoon tea and kicked up a fuss. He said he was a Ladbrooks shareholder, the London owners of the Hilton chain. 'We wondered if he was perhaps a little disappointed when he discovered we really were not part of his chain. We never worried too much about the name causing any trouble. It would always be good publicity for us, and Blackball.'

Blackball and its celebrated hotel have been thriving. Catering for casual visitors and backpackers, Formerly The Blackball Hilton is frequently booked up in advance. And the town provides an idyllic haven for its population of 400, many of whom still live in old mining cottages and cook on well-blackened coal ranges. At weekends Blackball frequently becomes a hideaway for increasing numbers of high-profile Christchurch people.

But when I caught up with Jane and Linda in May 2000, almost exactly five years after my first visit, Jane said nobody seemed keen to buy their old hotel. But, with most of her attention on making swords and shields for a forthcoming medieval night, she was not too worried. They would still be proprietors when the 2000 Midwinter BlackballZup was held. The event involves three-member teams competing in a genuine pub crawl: with padded hands and knees, they crawl from pub to pub. At each stop they participate in gumboot throwing and other typically West Coast games.

'We've had a lot of fun,' Jane said. 'But Linda wants to go back to Christchurch to be closer to her daughter and ageing mother, and I need a new challenge. But I'll stay in Blackball. I love this hard-case town. I'll miss the saxophone player, but whoever gets to own Formerly The Blackball Hilton is likely to have our formerly Blackball sausage on the menu. We can put on the best salami sausages anywhere.'

CHAPTER 4

CHARACTERS OF THE COAL SEAMS

*My brother Frank was also a rope boy but
he didn't last long. He was a cracker piper
so he needed all his fingers.*

Jock Annan

In 1993 Jock and Shirley Annan were living in a small yellow cottage in Hector, just across the river from Granity. Jock, a long-retired coal miner who had emigrated from Scotland, remembered 1929 as the year when the big earthquake rocked the Buller — and much of the South Island. It was also the year his father bought him a pair of boots. But he couldn't wear them: his bare feet had become too hard from running along the railway line to school.

'We were living at Seddonville then. My father, a dour old Scot, was working up at the Stockton coal mine and came home once a fortnight with his pay. Next time he came home he said, "I'd better have a look at Jock's boots. They might want fixing."

'"Wheeerr's your booots?" he asked in his broad Scots accent. I told him I didn't have them — I'd swapped them for a Boy Scout knife. Next thing I get six laceholes up my backside. My father, he had no sense of humour.'

The little cottage, close to the sea about 30 kilometres north of Westport, almost shook from the laughter as Jock finished his story. Having spent the best part of a lifetime involved with coal mining on the West Coast, Jock and Shirley had experienced many hardships and, sometimes, tragedy, but their stories were often spiced with humour, and loud laughter accompanied almost every anecdote.

Just an hour earlier we had all been strangers. Now I was experiencing wonderful old-fashioned West Coast hospitality as we sat comfortably at the kitchen table. Everything around us was as neat as a pin. In the next room a tortoiseshell cat slept, unperturbed. Its name was Hope:

Jock and Shirley Annan in their Hector cottage in 1993.

Jock and Shirley would hope their cat would always make it safely across the main road outside the front door.

Through a kitchen window the view was of the aerial ropeway carrying Stockton coal down to the Ngakawau bins to be crushed and loaded into trains for export from Lyttelton. But my attention was drawn to a photograph album on the table as Shirley offered yet another slice of her excellent apple cake.

Jock was recovering from a stroke. Talking, he said, was good therapy. He was five when his family came to New Zealand from Scotland. They were coal miners — and champion pipers. 'In 1925 a cobber of my father's had written from New Zealand: "Come out here — this is good mining. The coal seams are 30 feet thick."

'My father said, "That's not mining: that's quarrying." Coal seams in Scotland were 18 inches to 2 feet thick and you had to lie on your side in the mine.'

The young Annan had been known as John until he arrived on the West Coast but he was christened Jock by the children at Westport School because he turned up wearing a kilt on his first day. In 1937, when he was 16 — he said they couldn't teach him anything at school — he joined

Characters of the Coal Seams

his father working at Stockton among the hills high above his present Hector home. As a rope boy, his job was to put the coal tubs on a running rope for emptying down at the tumbler, and take the empty ones off again. It was a job that cost many men a finger or two, ripped off after becoming jammed in the running rope. 'My brother Frank was also a rope boy but he didn't last long. He was a cracker piper so he needed all his fingers. He left the Coast to compete in the world piping championships in Scotland and came third.'

Jock turned the album pages to show one of the squat electric locomotives working on a 3-foot gauge railway that ran at Stockton from 1908 till about 1953 when it was replaced by the present aerial system. They were the first electric railway locomotives to be used in New Zealand. Built in the United States by the General Electric Company for mines all over the world, some were fitted with a rubber curtain suspended over the driver's open seat to insulate his head from the live overhead trolley wire.

An old Dodge bus, loaded with mine workers, crosses the railway at Stockton. Reg Merritt, seen at left, was a mechanic living at Stockton. His last job of the day was to lift the trolley wire, enabling the bus to pass underneath. (Photograph courtesy of Jock Annan)

'Our locomotives didn't have a rubber curtain so you had to be careful when you stood up,' Jock recalled. He became a brakesman, and then a driver on the 5.5-mile (about 8.3-kilometre) railway that hauled trains of coal tubs between the mine and the steep ropeway that carried the tubs from Stockton down to the Ngakawau bins. There were two tunnels — one over a kilometre long — and 1 in 12 grades with centre—rail braking.

Working on the trains was no soft option for a miner. It required a certain amount of skill, and nerve. Sometimes a three-link coupling would break, setting adrift some of the 20 or so tubs in the rake. If the train stopped while descending from the mine, then the loaded breakaways would catch up, often with a predictable devastating crash. Runaways resulting from a brakesman's failure to grip the centre rail were also a cause of considerable havoc. Men riding in the tubs often lost fingers, or bits of their heads, in the pile-ups.

'One day in 1946 a driver was on the job drunk and we started to run back. It was going too fast for me to jump off and, being at the back of the train, I knew that any attempt to brake would have everything going over the top of me. It was just after three in the afternoon when the back-shift miners were queuing to collect their pay. They heard this thing coming and took off. Hundreds of pounds in bank notes were left scattered everywhere. Next thing the driver at the other end of the train got his brake to grip at the end of centre rail. The couplings tightened and I was shanghaied into a flax bush.'

Jock showed a photograph of a train leaving the tunnel in the Fly Creek section, with Jim Fogarty, a brakesman, standing on the loco. One day Jock found him dead. He was lying on top of a blacksmith's anvil beside the railway. 'He was Irish, and his mother's accent was as broad as a plank.' The doctor, concerned that Jim had died without making a Will, asked if he had died intestate. '"Well if Jim was here," his mother replied, "then he'd be able to tell you for his own self!"'

Another Irishman worried incessantly about burglars, so he bought himself a six-shooter which he took to bed with him. Waking up one night, he thought he heard someone trying to break in. He fired the gun, blowing off his big toe. A few weeks later, and out of hospital, his mates in the pub said, 'That was bad luck, Paddy.' 'Oh no,' replied Paddy, 'If I had been sleeping with my head at the other end of the bed, I'd have blown my brains out!'

When they married, Jock and Shirley lived up at Number One Loop, a small settlement at Stockton known as Tin Town because everything

Jim Fogarty standing on one of Stockton's electric locomotives working on the Fly Creek section. One day Jock Annan found him dea, lying on a blacksmith's anvil. (Photograph courtesy Jock Annan)

was made from corrugated iron. There was no road in those days. Everyone, including women and children, had to walk up the hill through the railway tunnels. The miners went to work in the coal tubs, and returned home sitting on the coal. More often than not, they were drenched by the pouring rain. If someone died they were taken down in a coal tub. There was a special tub for the post office, with a coat of arms painted on each side. Another, with locked doors across the top, carried groceries and other provisions.

'We had everything we wanted,' said Shirley. 'We had our movie theatre, tennis courts and swimming baths. Then there were the dance social evenings, and school committees. We caught freshwater crayfish in the creeks. You made your own life up there. Our three children enjoyed growing up at Stockton.' Jock recalled popping the small freshwater crayfish into the billy of tea. 'They came out nicely cooked,' he laughed.

Power for the town, supplied from the 275 volt DC trolley wire, was disconnected after the last train, sometime after midnight, and the backshift miners went home to eat their supper by candlelight. Jock recalled the night he set the house on fire.

'This particular night I arrived home to Tin Town and went inside through the back door into the kitchen. Unknown to me, the flame of my miner's head lamp had set alight my father's coat hanging behind the door. 'I was having a cup of tea when the power went off. To my surprise the hallway remained lit up. '"Hey Dad!" I shouted. "The house's on fire!" Next thing, in his long-johns, no teeth and his large handlebar moustache, he looked quite a sight with Mum over his shoulder. She was a big woman but Dad managed to chuck her out the window. We then put out the fire.'

Jock said his father had a thing about fires after that. About a month later Jock was home after being on back shift again. His brother called to see him and share a slice or two of toast before the power went off.

'I was telling my brother about Rowdy Thompson. He was so rowdy you couldn't hear him when he talked. They had Rowdy firing shots that night. You should have heard him when he shouted "FIRE", I said, trying to imitate Rowdy. Just then my father was up. "Oh no, not another bugger!" and before we could stop him, Mum was chucked out the window again.'

Jock described his father as a big man, six feet in his stockinged feet. Before migrating to New Zealand he was a proud member of the Royal Highland Regiment, known as the Black Watch. Jock did not find it easy getting on with his father, and he was impossible to work with in the mine.

When I asked Jock how his father reacted to his setting the house on fire. Jock merely replied, 'Oh, he took a dim view of it.'

Jock led the way to his garage, and his 0-gauge model railway. He had built a Denver and Rio Grande 4-8-4 Northern locomotive. In another part of his garage he had a lathe he used for various small engineering jobs, including making parts for 0-gauge models of the quaint rounded-iron coal tubs for a souvenir shop at Stockton. He was popular with local people wanting small engineering jobs done. It was once easy to get such jobs done over at the Ngakawau workshop, but not any longer. 'I'll tell you how bad it is,' he said. 'There was a time when old people who had worked in the mines for years would take a trailer across to the bins and get fixed up with coal. You can't do that any longer, export coal's too expensive.'

The building where electric power was once steam-generated for the Stockton electric railway still stands across at Ngakawau, not far from the Annans' cottage. Today it is minus its tall chimney that was necessary to take away the coal smoke.

'They couldn't get men to paint the chimney in those days. Nobody had the nerve to go up there. So they used to advertise in the papers when overseas coal ships were in Westport. The riggers, it was no trouble for them. They would put the bosun's chair up there, and up they'd go. They used to do the job, and at their own price too! The coal miners, by comparison, always got a rum deal. We had to pay for everything, even the explosives we used.'

Jock and Shirley insisted I stay on for tea. It was early July, and Jock had just dug a bucket of new potatoes. He asked if I would share a whisky, and talked about a lifelong interest in railways. He had a large collection of American railroad videotapes. His parents were worried when they lost him at Waterloo Station on their way out to New Zealand all those years ago. Jock, aged five, was eventually found in the cab of the locomotive No. 4462, the Flying Scotsman that had hauled their train from Edinburgh.

Another interest was country music, especially the Jimmy Rodgers railroad songs. After tea, he picked up his guitar for the first time since his stroke, and soon gained his confidence while strumming the strings. Then, adding his voice, we heard passable renditions of 'The Wreck of Old 97' and 'Hobo Bill's Last Ride'

> *Riding on an east-bound freight train*
> *Speeding through the night*
> *Hobo Bill, the railroad bum*
> *Lay fighting for his life . . .*

Then the conversation returned to the old days at Stockton as Jock recalled Dr Jim Simpson, the mine's doctor. 'My father had his head split open by a large piece of sharp coal. I remember him yelling with pain as the doctor put iodine in the wound and cleaned it out with a scrubbing brush. The doctor said that was to prevent him being tattooed with coal dust as the wound healed.'

On another occasion, a miner had died when a coal fall had removed much of his face. Jock recalled him being bandaged up like a mummy. 'Dr Simpson asked me to help him with the body and when I started to squirm he said, "Hurry up boy, this fellow won't hurt you."'

Money was taken from the miners to cover medical expenses and kept in a jar in the doctor's clinic. One day two miners helped themselves, and the police were called in. 'The two were caught, but Dr Simpson bailed them out and got them off the hook. He was that sort of fellow. One of them had a short memory, however. He got himself in an influential position and made it clear it was time to employ a younger doctor. Dr Simpson was fired during the 1950s.'

Happier memories were of nights spent driving the small electric locomotives. 'It was beautiful in the moonlight. With so many trains, the rails shone silver, and the wire used to hum with the trolley. I used to love that sound — and seeing the sparks off the wheels too.'

Jock and Shirley left the West Coast for Christchurch when the electric railway was soon to be replaced by the aerial cableway. 'I left for the family's sake,' Jock told me and I detected a sadness in his voice. 'I got a job driving trucks. One day, going down Moorhouse Avenue, I was

Coal miners riding to work aboard a rake of coal tubs.
(Photograph courtesy Jock Annan)

driving this old water cart used for roadworks when the steering wheel came off. I then got a job driving the old Bagnal loco at the New Zealand Refrigerating Company. We couldn't afford a house. All our friends, and the whitebait, were over on the other side of the mountains. I never liked Christchurch, unless I was looking at it in my rear-vision mirror, leaving for the Coast.'

The evening wore on, and even as I was about to drive off West Coast hospitality was again to the fore. Shirley said, 'Just a minute, don't go yet.' I waited until she returned with a large packet of frozen whitebait. She had caught it herself.

Sometime during May 2000 I rang Shirley. 'I lost Jock two years ago this August,' she told me. 'All that coal dust on his lungs. His heart couldn't take it any longer. They called it miners' disease. It's how so many coal miners ended up.

'One night he just said he wanted to go to bed. He went into the bathroom and when he came out he collapsed against the wall. I said, "Steady on, man." He then took off and collapsed and died in his favourite chair. Yes, it was a great shock.'

'He took a great memory of Scotland and the West Coast with him. He became a Kiwi over the years but he still kept some of his Scottish ideas. He always said when he retired he would go back and look at Scotland. But we never did.'

Jock Annan, aged 75, died on 9 August 1998. Shirley wanted to stay in their neat yellow cottage. 'But to carry on living here I had to learn to drive the car. So at 75 I got my first driver's licence. I had a good patient instructor,' she laughs. 'And, oh yes, I'm still whitebaiting, but my back's playing up a bit now.'

CHAPTER 5
HOKITIKA'S SEVEN WONDERS

Similar people were likely to have existed in any other New Zealand town, but no other town had quite the same romantic history of a gold rush.

Jim Keenan

Seven illustrious characters who were prominent in the life of Hokitika during the 1930s and 1940s have a special place in West Coast folklore. Known, somewhat facetiously, as the Seven Wonders of Hokitika, they preserve a time-honoured West Coast tradition for engendering the unusual.

'They were all celebrities in one way or another,' says Jim Keenan, a one-time Hokitika deputy mayor, taxi proprietor, and holder of several other key positions in the town. 'More so than elsewhere, Hokitika of the 1930s and 1940s was run by people who were well endowed with common-sense rather than professional qualifications. Living in an isolated part of New Zealand they had to be adaptable and they could turn their hand at anything.'

Jim Keenan is custodian of Hokitika's seven wonders. Aged 70-something, and the archetypal Coaster, he claims to be neither old, nor ancient, but he has a love of history. He is a member of the Historic Places Trust regional committee and was its chairman for many years.

His grandfather on his mother's side was Harry Gaylor, one of Hokitika's first settlers, who arrived from Melbourne in 1864. Having set up profitable businesses in Australia, he set out to do the same in Hokitika. He established the Marquis of Lorne Hotel in Hampden Street, which was soon regarded as the civilised area of the West Coast. Another Gaylor hotel, the Royal Mail in Woodstock, is still going. Other business establishments included a blacksmith's shop, a billiard saloon, a butchery and a drapery.

Jim Keenan is guardian of the Seven Wonders of Hokitika.

'This was Woodstock's first shopping mall, if you like. He raised a family of five daughters and one son. He had followed the gold rush to Woodstock, built two dams, and sold water to miners. For anyone down on his luck my grandfather was the one person to dodge. He was the one man they were likely to owe money to. Thus there was an insolvents' track to Woodstock. It bypassed the Royal Mail Hotel.'

Because Jim Keenan was brought up in a hotel, he was able to meet and get to know all those people who are included in the Seven Wonders of Hokitika. 'Whenever we're talking about people from the old days someone is bound to say, "Of course, he was one of the Seven Wonders of Hokitika." No one knows for sure who compiled the Seven Wonders. You know how we see the Seven Wonders of the World — the Hanging Gardens of Babylon, the Pyramids and all that — well, I suppose somebody with a streak of humour suggested we have the Seven Wonders of Hokitika.'

Heading the list is 'Doc' Andrews, custodian of the Hokitika swimming baths for many years even though he could not swim a stroke. 'I remember him walking with a swinging gait — he must have had a problem with his hip. He was a great character who used to rule the baths which were always spotlessly clean. The kids all got on well with him because they knew where they stood. If Doc asked them to do something they would jump to it.'

Then there was Donald McLeod, the Lightning Calculator, who could neither read or write, but could almost instantly give the answer to any mathematical problem, or calculate how many times the town clock had struck over a given period.

'Donald had a deformed face that badly affected his speech. He could multiply, say, 2538.1 by 17.96, and give you the answer accurately and simply. He became a bit of a national celebrity when Micky Spiers set up Greymouth's first radio station. In Hokitika a branch station was run by the hairdresser and local musician, Albert Lawn — known to listeners as Uncle Albert — and he often had Donald on air.

'No matter how hard they tried, nobody was able to trick Donald. When he gave an almost instant answer to someone asking how many times the Hokitika clock had chimed over a certain period in 1945, one listener challenged Donald, saying he was short by 15 or 20. Donald then cited the days when the clock had been shut down and didn't chime. A check through the borough records proved him to be correct, as was usually the case.'

Hokitika's War Memorial clock in the centre of town is the subject of a Seven Wonders story involving Donald McLeod, the 'Lightening Calculator'.

Billy Gaylor, a distant relation of Jim Keenan, is said to have been one of Hokitika's best borough employees because he successfully held down so many jobs, including inspector of nuisances, keeper of the pound and chief traffic officer. A short, efficient man, he is remembered as 'Willie Ever Grow, the traffic officer who couldn't drive a car and always rode a bicycle'.

'They say he was really effective. There were plenty of cars around by the 1940s and Billy Gaylor pulled them up from his bicycle. I remember him quite well and the funny way he had of getting on his bicycle. There was an extension from the back axle to put his foot on and he mounted over the seat from the back rather than put his leg over the bar. He was such a little fellow.'

Hokitika is said to have had the only TAB where you could bet 'on tick'. Ernie Heenan, the mayor of the day and TAB agent, was known as Tick Heenan. 'At the corner store, and even in the hotel, people got 'tick' but I doubt if anyone really got credit at the TAB, even on the West Coast — the rules would not have allowed it.'

Garney Howe, who died about 15 years ago, is remembered as the harbourmaster who had never been to sea. In its heyday Hokitika would have as many as 50 ships in port at the one time. During 1866 and 1867 Hokitika exported the highest value of cargo from any New Zealand port. Ten tons of gold went out over the Hokitika River bar in just one year.

'By the 1940s when Garney was harbourmaster the port was starting to decline. He is regarded as being the only harbourmaster, anywhere, who had never been to sea, but he ran the waterfront efficiently until the late 1960s when Hokitika's port closed.

'He is also remembered as the Silver Pine King of Westland because of his dealing with timber for fence posts. One day a Canterbury farmer came over to buy 1000 silver-pine posts. Before making the purchase he said, "But are they any good, Mr Howe?" "Any good!" replied Garney, "silver pine will last for ever, and if it's treated it will last for longer!"'

George Burt was the motor-garage proprietor who, like the traffic officer, could not drive a car. Having been a marine engineer, he set up Ross & Burt in the centre of town near the memorial clock. It then became Thomas Bros Garage for many years. 'One of the more recent principals told me that his brother was an apprentice when George Burt ran the place. He got quite a shock when he discovered that the apprentice had to drive his employer whenever there was a breakdown. I suppose, being a marine engineer, he never had the opportunity, or need, to drive a car.'

A brewer could hardly escape being included in the Seven Wonders. George McIntosh, who is better remembered as 'Geo Mac', had never tasted a glass of beer in his life, yet he was widely regarded as a top brewer. 'He was a nice old fellow; a Shetland Islander with a fine handlebar moustache, and an unusual lilt to his voice. He was a respected member of the community, and as far as I know he never drank at all.'

Jim Keenan says that over the years when one of the people dropped off the list, another has been added. He agrees that similar people were likely to have existed in any other New Zealand town, but no other town had quite the same romantic history of a gold rush.

'The New Zealand writer and historian Ross Gore said that the rise of Hokitika was even more dramatic than San Francisco. We seem to have come from nothing — not one person — early in 1864 and by 1867 Hokitika was a rollicking town some historians have claimed reached as high as 80,000, even though it was more like 30,000 to 40,000.'

The first thoroughfare, Revell Street, was marked out in December 1864. By early 1865 Hokitika displayed all the usual features of a big gold rush: drinking, fighting, and gambling to the extreme.

'Most gold seekers came from Victoria. Champagne Charlies were here by the score as the traditional gold diggers' extravagance was continued in Hokitika. Timber and canvas buildings lined either side of Revell Street, and every other building was dignified by the name of a hotel. They were Hokitika's "brave old days". We also had dance halls with posh names: the Casino de Venise and Montezuma. Dancing girls were imported from Melbourne.'

As gold poured out of Hokitika — more than 52,000 ounces during the first five months of 1865 — so the town grew. The extent of that growth is evident in the Harnett and Co.'s *West Coast Gold Fields Directory* of 1866. 'To consider the whole string of businesses, including barristers and solicitors, accountants, and schools and other facilities in Hokitika by that year is astonishing. How could an isolated West Coast town where rain was heavy and where forests reached down to the sea, have developed so quickly? Just imagine going down to a remote Fiordland river today and developing a town like Hokitika of the mid-1860s. Even with all the money in the world you would be flat stick to do it in just one year.'

In recent times the search for gold has been revived as modern machinery turns over a portion of Hokitika's surrounding countryside for one last time. Gold is once again contributing to the local economy, as is tourism. Visitors frequently depart Hokitika impressed by the small town (population about 4000) with a commercial airport and a number of enterprising businesses, especially those along Tancred Street working with jade, wood, glass and gold. These, and a genuine French café, Café de Paris, are perhaps the modern wonders of Hokitika — along with the autumn Wildfoods Festival. Arguably the greatest Kiwi culinary event, the festival attracts thousands of South Islanders who gleefully wash down some of the world's quirkiest foods with the local Monteith's brew, gumboot milkshakes, gorseflower wine or genuine bushman's billy tea.

And on a fine day, almost every south-facing street offers a stunning view of Mounts Cook and Tasman. Even as the town evolves, stories of the old characters as depicted in the Seven Wonders of Hokitika will define a West Coast image those of us living east of the Southern Alps have grown to love.

'The Seven Wonders of Hokitika is a facetious sort of arrangement that never fails to make a good talking point,' says Jim Keenan. 'I remember walking into the Red Lion one evening when a character, Jim Symons, was running the hotel. He said, "Jim, tell these visitors about the Seven Wonders of Hokitika" so I recited them and when I had finished he said, "You're wrong you know; there's eight."

'I said, "Who's the eighth?" and he said that he was.

'I said, "How do you qualify?" To this Jim proudly told us across the bar that he was the only Protestant to have been president of the St Mary's School Committee.'

BORN TO BE WILD

Hokitika's idiosyncrasies are to the fore when the annual Wildfoods Festival dishes up some of the best gourmet bush tucker anywhere. Each autumn Hokitika's population swells four-fold when more than 15,000 visitors descend on the town looking for a culinary experience that embraces the unusual and the quirky.

They are never disappointed. Regular treats include gourmet huhu grubs and garden worms, along with westcargots (local snails cooked in white wine), possum stew and all bull bits — testicles, brains and spleen — possum pies, king prawns, 1080 cookies, sphagnum candyfloss and brandy snaps filled with wild berries and cream. 'A few years ago we wouldn't have thought people would eat worms or snails but they took to them like pigs to strawberries,' says festival organiser Mike Keenan. 'One year we had octopus testicles. I didn't know they had them!'

The festival had its origins in genuine old West Coast hospitality. 'A Coaster would go out and shoot a deer or rabbit, catch a possum, or collect mussels from rocks in the sea. He would then share his bush

Co-ordinator of the Hokitika Wildfood Festival, Mike Keenan says he is promoting a unique extravaganza of food and West Coast hospitality. 'Nowhere else will you get the old coaster. He's as honest as hell. One day a year he dresses up and really puts it on.'

Born to be Wild

Preparing and eating food you wouldn't want to eat at home — huhu grubs at the Hokitika Wildfoods Festival. (Photographs courtesy Mike Keenan)

food with his friends. These days, of course, everything has to be balanced with MAF regulations to ensure the quality of wild food.'

The Hokitika Wildfoods Festival is enthusiastically supported by the famous West Coast Monteith's Brewery, whose brews mix particularly well with whitebait patties. In 1990 the inaugural festival began as a small event, attracting just 25 stalls and about 1800 people. But the idea caught on, and local wildfoods were mixed with international flavours, representing the 1860s gold rush immigrants. So the festival goer is likely to find fare such as crocodile and kangaroo, haggis and even a wildfoods sushi made to a special West Coast recipe of smoked eel, whitebait, watercress and wasabi.

Notable South Islanders to attend the festival have included former Prime Minister Jenny Shipley, who was a guest reader at Live Poets' Corner during the 1998 festival. And the poetry star of 1999 was the United States-born storyteller Mary-Alice Arthur who arrived in New Zealand about 17 years ago to launch event tourism with the New Zealand Tourism Board. Although she has become an honorary Wellingtonian, she nevertheless discovered a delightful similarity between the archetypal West Coast character, and the world of the lumberjacks she grew up with. All larger-than-life characters, they were not unlike those who moulded the traditions and folklore of the South Island's West Coast.

CHAPTER 6

A PASSION FOR PLANES AND PIZZA

I enjoy doing spur-of-the-moment things as so easily you fall into the dullness of routine.

Terry Lee

Terry Lee, an Australian from Melbourne, wrote to tell me he had read my book *Journeying with Aviators*. Despite having an artificial leg he started to fly himself and, in mid-life, struggled to obtain his Private Pilot Licence. He enjoyed his flying, there was no doubt about that, and he also had a way with words. The culinary delight of his life, best enjoyed after a day's flying, was a superb pizza.

But as I read on I started to discover the real reason for his long, compelling letter: more than anything, he loved New Zealand's South Island. His one regret was that, learning to fly, meant he had not visited for more than two years.

'I have been to your South Island a dozen times and I fell in love with two places in particular; a quirky little town called Twizel near Mount Cook (I want to live there one day), and the South Westland glaciers with their little townships at Franz Josef and the Fox. I cherish these places for their splendid isolation. But I rather like the Maori description for the glaciers and surrounding mountains: "Tiritiri o te Moana". Better than the adopted European version. Tiritiri o te Moana, I have been assured, means "Vision of the Ocean".

'I once heard one of your countrymen describe the South Island as "the footprints of God". I agree. I should like one day to fly your majestic valleys and moraines . . .'

While staying in Hokitika (having first checked out the airfield overlooking the town), he was invited to a wedding. He did not know any of the people involved, but they were staying at the same motel. 'I got talking to this guy who happened to be the bride's father. To my delight and astonishment he invited me to the wedding, and sat me at the main table. 'I loved every minute of it. I generally do not drink (except for a Liqueur Muscat or an aged Tokay) but that night I got plastered. They kept filling my glass. What an absolute hoot. I was dreadfully hung over the next day and in no condition to drive, or even walk! I've never met any of those wonderful people since.'

Eventually I answered Terry's letter, sending him clippings of newspaper stories I had written about flying, and stories about one or two of my own South Island antics. The correspondence continued. He

The roof of New Zealand, Mount Tasman 3496 metres (left) and Mount Cook 3754 metres, and the Cook River flowing away from Fox Glacier. They are viewed from a ski-plane flight soon after take-off from the Fox airstrip.

wrote long accounts of adventurous cross-country flights in Australia, taking off from a humble strip at the Sunbury Aero Club. I did not always read his letters immediately, but put them aside, sometimes for several days, until I could savour them, invariably with a glass of good wine. Reading about Terry and his passion for flying and the South Island could not be hurried.

'Yes, I am permanently broke, money is related to hours back in the air and I live a hermit's life during the week waiting to be able to fly on the weekends. When I fly I am free. I am living a dream.'

Every so often he would include a snippet about the South Island. He once spent six weeks staying at Twizel. 'I enjoy Twizel because it's relatively isolated, definitely quiet, not many tourists seem to stay there and, importantly, everyone is very friendly. I loved getting up before dawn and walking away from the township to watch the sun rise. When it snows, the Ben Ohau range flanking the town becomes a wonderland. I would simply stop at each place, at Twizel and the glaciers for days, even weeks, on end and more or less go nowhere else. Every time I visit New Zealand I always make a point of travelling only to the South Island. Nothing wrong with your North Island, but the two are incomparable.

Guided party on Franz Josef glacier.

Haruko Morita, from Japan, enjoys a close encounter with ice flowing from the Franz Josef glacier.

'By the way, there is a great pizza shop in the Fox Glacier township. As you travel south it's on the left opposite the post boxes. Best pizzas in Aussie or New Zealand.' He then told me about a time when the desire for a pizza was so strong that he made a completely unplanned trip to New Zealand, hopping on an Air New Zealand flight one Friday after work. 'I arrived in Christchurch about 2 o'clock in the morning, hired a car and drove to Fox via Arthur's Pass. I had my pizza and immediately drove back to Christchurch to catch my return flight to

Melbourne. I was in time for work on Monday morning. I enjoy doing spur-of-the-moment things as so easily you fall into the dullness of routine.'

His letter went on to relate another highlight during a visit to South Westland when he spent two days exploring the upper névés of one of the glaciers and was eventually picked up by helicopter. It sounded magical but my thoughts remained stuck on the pizza story. 'I just hope the shop is still there,' he wrote in yet another long letter. 'Mmmmm, I can just smell the pizza right now, and I can hear the soundtrack music from the movie *The Mission* playing, as it was back then.'

Was the pizza shop still there? Nothing in the telephone directory suggested it was. So I decided to go there, having met up with my Japanese friend Haruko in Greymouth. We hired a car and set off. If there was no pizza shop, at the very least I could walk with Haruko to the terminal face of the Franz Josef Glacier. We did this, going as close as we dared to the enormous ice cave.

Later, I told Haruko the story of the Maori name for the Franz Josef; Ka Roimata o Hine Hukatere, meaning 'flowing tears of Hine Hukatere'. Hine Hukatere, a beautiful Maori maiden, was a mountaineer — her name can be translated as 'moving ice' — who took her boyfriend onto the glacier. He was not a climber, but Hine Hukatere made him chase her around the mountains until he fell into a crevasse and was killed. Hine Hukatere was so grief-stricken that the gods allowed her tears to become frozen into the glacier.

I also introduced Haruko to one of those wonderful West Coast culinary delights: a whitebait patty washed down by Monteith's Original beer. And we drove on to the Fox.

In the township one place stood out as matching Terry Lee's description, the Café Névé, opposite the post boxes. And the story of the pizza-loving Aussie was accepted with the appropriate smiles and looks of amazement. Café Névé (previously the Cone Rock Café) is still making wonderful pizzas in South Westland. One was created especially for my photograph and then it was suggested that Haruko and I sample it.

'We make our own pizza bases and cook them in a special oven,' one of the staff, Nigel Bain, assured me. Our medium continental gourmet pizza was certainly good and went down equally well with the Kiwi and Japanese palates. Haruko and I listed the ingredients and tastes:

Mel Brown and Nigel Bain with a gourmet pizza at the Café Névé in the Fox township. They're worth a special trip — from Melbourne, or even Tokyo.

smoked sausage, salami (presumably from Blackball), tomato paste (homemade, Nigel told us), plenty of mozzarella cheese, onion, garlic, red and green peppers, olives and sesame seeds. I suspect we missed a few.

'But would you make a special trip from Melbourne — or Tokyo — just for a pizza like this?' I asked Haruko. Her delightful face broke into laughter. 'Maybe I would,' she said.

Closer to Home

CHAPTER 7

DEFENDER OF THE PORT HILLS

*My grandfather told stories about how he
appreciated the environment. I suppose I
have been burdened with this same love.*
                              Gordon Kirk

Gordon Kirk, my neighbour, fell from his roof and smashed his right ankle. It was Christmas Eve about four years ago, but I can still hear the anguished cry of pain and the sound of a metal ladder crashing on stone. I was hanging out the washing when it happened. Dropping everything and rushing next door, I arrived at the twisted body about the same time as Ellen, Gordon's wife. Somehow we got him inside and made him as comfortable as possible before Ellen called the doctor.

My neighbour's Christmas wasn't much fun that year, and it would be some time before I would once again enjoy his quirky humour and see that slow, knowing smile spread across his face. But another drama was to follow.

In the hospital, X-rays showed a painful collection of shattered bones in Gordon's ankle. (Few parts of the body have such a complicated bone structure.) The orthopaedic surgeon said he would need to fuse the bones. Luckily, however, he went on holiday and another surgeon, knowing Gordon Kirk's love for walking on the Port Hills overlooking Christchurch, said he would have to do better. What followed was a complex operation involving screwing bones to a metal plate so that the ankle was reassembled into something emulating the original.

'I'm forever grateful to that surgeon,' my 74-year-old neighbour told me as we climbed a track named after him on the western flank of the hills. 'My ankle's as good as new. I can keep up with anyone. Had the bones been fused, I would have been looking for new interests.'

He has been a member of the Summit Road Society for 30 odd years and was its president for five, leading the society's unsuccessful opposition to building the Mount Cavendish Gondola on a piece of land believed to have been protected by the Reserves Act. His passion for the Port Hills and their ultimate preservation might be compared to that of Harry Ell who pioneered the Summit Road early this century. Ell's legacy is the road and a series of wonderful stone roadhouses that include the Sign of the Takahe, the Sign of the Kiwi, and the Sign of the Bellbird.

Gordon Kirk has taken a different tack. He has worked to have more land placed under preservation, and opened up for recreation by constructing walking tracks. In October 1998 his name appeared on a sign marking a new walking track through Omahu Bush on the western side of the hills. Kirk's Track descends about 300 metres from Cass Peak and Gordon helped to build it with a small group of volunteers working one day a week for a year. Wryly he says he was not the leader of the gang — 'No one wanted to take responsibility for that' — but admits that his group could be reminiscent of *The Last of the Summer Wine*. 'We enjoyed the companionship and we found time to sit around and tell stories. For all that, we amazed ourselves how quickly we could get things done. The track looks simple enough now, but there were plenty

Gordon Kirk pauses to enjoy the Mount Pleasant Bluffs Track overlooking Lyttelton Harbour. He is 'burdened by a love of nature', inherited from his grandfather.

of boulders and places to fall off. It was in the back of our minds that if one of us did fall we would have to attend a funeral. That would have unnecessarily delayed work on the track.'

Anne Henderson, who spent 15 years as the Summit Road Society's secretary, says Gordon Kirk has done a tremendous amount of background work towards the ultimate preservation of the Port Hills, more so than many others of his generation. 'He always finds out what land will be for sale, and he tirelessly works with landowners to get permission for walking tracks to cross their land. He's also prepared all the material for hearings whenever encroaching developers threatened to change the nature of the Port Hills.'

But Gordon Kirk does not think he is anything special. 'A lot of others have worked hard for the preservation of the Port Hills, people like the botanists Arnold Wall and Dr Leonard Cockayne.' He also talks about the contribution made by John Jameson, Harry Ell's grandson and fellow member of the Summit Road Society. If he has an obsession for the Port Hills then it is a selfish one. 'I do it all for my own pleasure. I get more out of what I do than anyone else does.'

Gordon Kirk was not born under the shadow of the Port Hills; he is from Waimate. His cousin Norman Kirk became leader of the Labour Party and, in 1972, Prime Minister of New Zealand. In Waimate he worked as a dairyman 'milking a couple of cows and delivering the milk around town in a billy'. With two older brothers he started the first South Island bulk milk tanker collection. All the while his passions were the environment — and music. In 1943 he had started an orchestra in Waimate, finding six people who could play. The orchestra soon expanded to 45 members and Ellen was among the aspiring violinists.

In 1953 he and Ellen established KB Dairies in Ashburton. They also pioneered work on farm-tank refrigeration. 'It was sheer hell,' Gordon recalls with a laugh. When they sold their interest in the dairy factory, the Kirks bought a property in Governors Bay and Gordon found an interest in landscape design and nursery work. Another career change saw Gordon and Ellen taking over the Alpine Motels at Arthur's Pass for 10 years. 'That was great. Life's a breeze up there in the mountains. But the ladies don't seem to like it so much.'

Returning to Christchurch, he opened a small music shop in the Arts Centre. He played the violin and trumpet but, he says, was never too good at either. 'I did have an understanding of the working of brass, woodwind and string instruments which I was able to put to good use.'

Rhodes Monument, a striking landmark above Mount Levy. The track leads to Mount Herbert, the highest point on Banks Peninsula.

He also did some 'interesting things no one else did', which included taking an expensive $300 recorder to the wood turner if it was slightly flat. 'You shorten the length a little and the pitch goes up.'

When the Christchurch Operatic Society staged Mozart's *The Magic Flute* some years ago a bad quality pan flute was sent over from Sydney. 'Christopher Doig, who was then the Arts Centre manager, came over and asked could I do anything with this tin whistle. I said I would make him a pan flute from wood by cutting down some small recorders.' So Gordon went to work with a hacksaw and tuned the recorders to the music. When it was all glued together it was very much like the real thing and also had an authentic sound. 'The lead singer who played Papageno said he was having it once the show was over.'

Gordon Kirk retired from his music shop a decade ago, and took over as president of the Summit Road Society when the gondola argument was in full swing.

'We lost members who believed the gondola idea had some merit. Our argument was against building the complex on land protected by the Reserves Act. The developers also rode rough shod over the Summit

Road Act Norman Kirk had put to Parliament in 1963 to enhance recreational opportunities. The intentions of both acts were undermined. But we have now got the gondola, so it's in everyone's interest that it works.

'We lost the battle with the gondola developers. But I think it made people realise the law doesn't necessarily give protection against indiscriminate developers.'

The gondola argument, he admits, is something he would rather not have been involved in. It involved a lot of time preparing submissions for hearings, and created considerable bad feeling. But the society was able to get involved in building the Mount Pleasant Bluffs Track on Department of Conservation land. Ironically, the new track started close to the gondola complex. 'The attention of Summit Road Society members was turned to a more positive role, creating one of the most exciting tracks on the Port Hills with views that are possibly unsurpassed on Banks Peninsula.'

Over the years Gordon Kirk has encouraged the Summit Road Society to buy blocks of land as they have become available, adding to the 140-

A stylish complex on the Port Hills, the Mount Cavendish gondola project went ahead following 1980s protest hearings initiated by the Summit Road Society. The gondola, opened in October 1992, is built on land that was believed to have been protected by the Reserves Act.

hectare Ohinetahi Bush block already in the society's ownership. His vision is for the Port Hills to be recognised as a special area of national importance and shown on maps as a regional park. Already several landowners have recognised the value of their properties as conservation areas and want to contribute to a regional park concept. Omahu Bush, through which Kirk's Track has been built, is a good example. The land, once part of the Otahuna property, is owned by Grant and Marilyn Nelson but is administered by the Gama Foundation as a reserve. 'About 15 groups including councils have a stake in the future of the Port Hills.' Gordon talks fondly about his grandfather George Wilcox who went gold panning up Cape York way in north Queensland in the nineteenth century. 'He told stories about how he appreciated the environment. I suppose I've been burdened with this same love. In my case it's the Port Hills and being able to walk in open spaces, enjoying an outstanding landscape.'

If he has a particular regret it is the demise of the tuis on Banks Peninsula. There are plenty of theories, but he blames it on a big 1080 rabbit kill some years ago. 'They used raspberry jam for bait. Tuis would have discovered that a mile away. But too many people don't want to believe that was the case.'

Asked how he would have got on had he met up with Harry Ell, Gordon says he doesn't think he would have hit it off. 'I don't think I would have liked to have him on my patch. He was so obsessed with the Port Hills and that got him into a lot of trouble. Of course, if he wanted to build all those roadhouses today, maybe we wouldn't let him. We wouldn't agree to anyone building tearooms up along the Summit Road.'

He does agree that Ell had a wonderful vision for the Port Hills. 'And if something needed to be done, he just went ahead and did it. He didn't need to form a committee. I think the Summit Road Society has inherited some of Harry Ell's hands-on approach to getting things done. I think he just enjoyed what he was doing — as I am doing.'

During the latter part of 1999, when a busload of Summit Road devotees toured the Port Hills, someone suggested, 'We should pick the brains of Gordon Kirk and his mates before they go.' Gordon admits he may be losing some faculties but his hearing is not one of them. 'I wondered where they thought we were going, or how we were going,' he recalls with a knowing smile. 'For myself, I wasn't planning on going anywhere!'

HERALDIC TREASURES

A striking building at the Christchurch No. 2 bus terminus on Cashmere Hills has long been a curiosity. Styled on an old English coaching inn, the Sign of the Takahe stands as a legacy of the flamboyant politician and beautifier Henry (Harry) George Ell, arguably one of the most colourful South Island characters of the early 20th century.

This castle-like roadhouse contains New Zealand's largest and most comprehensive collection of heraldry. About 140 pieces include the shields of New Zealand governors, political figures, military people and many pioneer Canterbury families. Stained glass windows represent the Masonic fraternity, the shield of Prince John of Eltham and other striking imagery. The Scottish coat of arms and the English coat of arms are impressive ceiling pieces above the armorial (middle) room. And, topping the walls of the innermost room, historic friezes reflect periods of early English history from the conquests by the Romans and Normans,

The Sign of the Takahe on the Cashmere Hills stands as a striking memorial to the legendary, if eccentric, conservationist Harry Ell.

Prince John of Eltham Shield, Sign of the Takahe.

through to Lord Nelson. Despite its apparent randomness, it is a wonderful collection of colour and design. But that is the nature of the entire building, and its architecture, the result of Harry Ell's imagination.

'His desire was to emulate a grand early coaching stop,' says his grandson John Jameson. 'These days we see an impressive Tudoresque building on Cashmere Hills with tearooms and restaurant offering a full traditional silver service. It wasn't always like that. It was much less pretentious when it opened in 1919 as the tram terminus shelter, and when the first cups of tea were dispensed for one shilling.'

John Jameson, as much as anyone, helped to preserve the dreams of Harry Ell by founding the Summit Road Society in 1948. He was just a lad when his grandfather was working on his Summit Road project and recalls him being 'obsessed by the Summit Road along the Port Hills above Christchurch, and the future of its reserves and resthouses'.

The present stone building was completed by the Christchurch City Council in 1950, many years after Ell's death. Mary Douglas, Harry Ell's assistant and tearooms' manageress from the 1920s through to about 1941, was involved in the early heraldry work. 'We do not know who the artists were, but we believe they were from the ranks of the unemployed during the Depression years,' says John Jameson. 'The imagery was painted on all manner of scrap material such as petrol cases, butter boxes and old tea chests found in derelict Christchurch buildings.'

Heraldry has its origins in twelfth-century England and flourished through the Middle Ages, particularly on the battlefields where colourful surcoats, pendants and shields made a spectacle. With the invention of that great social leveller, gunpowder, heraldry disappeared from the battlefields to become a snobbish means to decorate property. The gentry paid a tax to have a coat of arms embossed on their carriages.

'The heraldry at the Sign of the Takahe is a commendable attempt to pay tribute to the founders of Canterbury,' says John Jameson. 'Hence the predominance of English and Scottish imagery. There are also shields of prominent New Zealand politicians and prime ministers — Savage, Semple and others. My grandfather would have known who to go to for help for his Summit Road concept. These shields may have been an acknowledgement.

'The Sign of the Takahe was my grandfather's most ambitious project. He saw much of the building completed, including the armorial room with its impressive ceiling artwork. Even on the night before he died in June 1934 he was anxious about the work on the Takahe . . . He was concerned with details about the quantity of gold leaf, stencils, or if he needed another sable brush.'

CHAPTER 8
LEGENDS AMONG THE ROCKS

> *When you go looking along the beaches you will see lots of white stones, and lots of coloured stones. Many of them will be green. But when you see jade, you will know straight away what it is.*
> — Hettie Feith-Wells

Hettie Feith-Wells lost a husband because of rocks. 'He said I was so obsessed with rocks, I should see a psychiatrist. I said, "Okay, if you come too," and that was the end of the marriage.'

For more than 30 years the delightfully cluttered Hettie's Rock Shop in Beckenham, Christchurch, was known to rockhounds round the world. It was the only shop of its kind in the South Island, and one of only three in New Zealand. Hettie collected rocks and fossils and sold them to make a living. And she learned the skills of lapidary, transforming her rocks into semi-precious stones and gemstones.

Hettie knew the stories and legends of rocks. From dealers she bought pieces of the prized purple crystals — known as amethyst — that for centuries had been buried beneath jungles in Brazil. She had green jasper with specks of red: that was one form of bloodstone. Another was the hematite. Whenever a piece of hematite is cut, the water turns red.

At one time her prized exhibit was a meteorite from South Africa, but this was upstaged when she carefully placed a dinosaur egg fossil from China in her shop. She loved agates, the fine-grained quartz polished to become beautiful gemstones. But she had a special connection with the dark green nephrite greenstone found on the South Island West Coast. Hettie became an authority on greenstone (or jade, as true rockhounds call it), and understood its mystique. And she gave many pieces to her friends. I always carry some of Hettie's jade. One is a small piece of flower jade that she once carried herself; another is a beautiful jade pebble from Barrytown Beach, north of Greymouth.

Hettie was born in West Java in 1925 to an old colonial Dutch family and brought up on a rubber plantation on the slopes of the volcano, Slamat. High-school classes at Bandung were multi-racial, but she could not recall any discrimination. The sultan's son went to the same school. As a schoolgirl she spent much of her spare time gazing at the wonderful display cases at the geological Museum of the Mines in Bandung, and collecting agates from the Tjitarum River. She once threw agates at a nasty male monkey that was watching her skinny-dipping. Asked why she was so sure of the monkey's sex she replied, 'Only a male would have shown such interest!'

The Japanese invaded Indonesia in 1942 when Hettie was aged 17 and she, like her mother and sister, spent the next three years in prisoner-of-war camps: Tjihapit, and then Lampersarie. Conditions for the women and children were as appalling as the brutality administered by the camp commandant. Almost 50 years later, Hettie had said little about her war years, but her two adult children began asking about her experiences.

'A lot has been written about the war but not about Indonesia, and even less about the fate of women and children in concentration camps. Those camps were really intended to exterminate people. The men were

Hettie Wells, a prolific collector of rocks.

of some use; they could become exchange prisoners, but we were nothing — an embarrassment even.

'The commandants went to war to win medals and honour. Those assigned to look after us felt dishonoured. Their resentment made them cruel. Then the Americans dropped the bomb on Hiroshima. We had no idea what had happened at Hiroshima. But suddenly we were given more food, and the cruelty stopped. The Japanese commandants suddenly disappeared.'

People had died needlessly, often as a result of severe punishment for attempting to steal food or make contact with the outside world. 'Many prisoners every day died towards the end of the war. The hospital was always full of people who were dead, but not yet dead. Each, in turn, was carried away in a bamboo coffin.'

Despite the harsh conditions, Hettie survived the war 'quite well,' having suffered little more than a few hard kicks, but her sister would die young. She attended school lessons in the camps — even though it was impossible to retain any information — and she became chief snake catcher.

'In the rubber plantations, poisonous snakes were always a problem with workers going about in bare feet. My mother became very proficient at treating snake bites. She would tie a tourniquet above the bite, make two criss-cross cuts with a razor blade and, once all the black poisonous blood had been squeezed out, she filled the cut with Condy's crystals.'

Recalling those war years Hettie was unable to understand the terrible things that can happen when one group has too much power over another. 'To me, that is the big why,' she said.

She was released from captivity, only to become embroiled in Indonesian problems. With her sister she was captured while out foraging for food. 'We had one bicycle we could load stuff on. We turned into a street where groups of Indonesians and Japs were screaming and yelling. The Indonesians were knocking down the Japs and capturing all the white people. We were caught with the others and made prisoners in an empty house. The Indonesians told us they would be back shortly and they said, "We will shoot you all, so say your prayers."

'Well, thank you very much, but nobody said his prayers. We all just tried to get out. Then we heard the rumbling of tanks. They were filled with Japanese soldiers, ordered by the British to protect white people. The Japanese released us from the house.'

After the war Hettie and her sister were sent to Holland to finish their education. To get there they had to sign on as crew on one of the repatriation ships. Hettie had spent only a short time in Holland when she was very young; it was almost a foreign country. 'It was cold, and crowded with narrow-minded people.'

Hettie married in 1948 and returned to Indonesia, but changes following the war made living there difficult for Dutch people, especially when Sukarno came to power. When she departed Indonesia for the second time she had to leave everything behind apart from her Bible, her silver, and a handful of agates. It was one of the occasions in her life when she knew what it was like to have almost nothing. 'The old colonial Dutch were a dying race. Those of us who came to New Zealand had to make the most of it. We couldn't go back to Indonesia, or Holland. We had burned all our bridges behind us.'

The only other choice would have been Australia — 'I might have gone to Queensland where it would have been warmer.' When I teased Hettie that she would never have discovered her nephrite jade, a smile appeared on her wonderful old face. 'Then I could have had all those opals and sapphires,' she replied. And she roared with laughter.

New Zealand was seen as a land of promise, a country where you could get a job if you wanted one, but Kiwis initially showed her little friendship. She arrived in Hamilton in January 1952 with her husband and small daughter. Another child was expected. At a block of flats where a home had been promised, Hettie and her family were forbidden to enter the front door; instead, they were taken through a gate to an old garden shed.

'Inside there was a double bed covered with a sack. We were told that was good enough for a migrant. They had no idea where we had come from, and we were thought to be dirty. How could I have explained that I had lived in a mansion with servants, and everything else, in Java?'

Getting work was also not easy in Hamilton, so the family moved to Christchurch where Hettie was recognised as one of New Zealand's first rockhounds. She was a founder of the Christchurch Rock Club and was soon amusing fellow members with her fledgling attempts at mastering the English language. In no time she became the local rock authority as she joined in club field trips to many parts of Canterbury and the West Coast. One day she discovered some unusual black and yellow agates in a landslide near Mount Somers. To this day the spot is known as Hettie's Slip.

When her first marriage broke up she decided to make a life for herself and start a rock shop. She had saved $500 which she thought would be enough. Having rented the building in Beckenham, and paid the cabinetmaker, she was $800 in debt. 'At the opening party on 30 April 1968, people were a bit apprehensive about my going into business. They asked if I knew what I was doing and I simply said, "No, I do not." I stocked the shop with my own collection of rocks and minerals. There were those I had collected in New Zealand and polished myself, and many I had swapped with other rockhounds all over the world.'

Soon after, she visited the bank manager to ask for a $500 loan. As a woman in business, and a foreigner, she had little chance. 'He sat up at this huge desk and looked down at me as if I was a speck of dirt. When he asked about my collaterals I told him I had no husband, no house and no car, but I did have a bicycle. He was not impressed.

'I was offered just $100, and he impressed on me it was only by the grace of God. I told him he could stick it, and went to a friend and borrowed the $500. It was paid back by Christmas and I also gave my friend a bottle of brandy as a bonus. I then had the audacity to go to the Shop Tribunal and ask for Saturday opening. This was granted because I was selling rocks to tourists, and no one opposed me.'

In 1971 Hettie married Bill Sawyers, a former assistant harbourmaster from Westport and keen rock collector. This time she enjoyed a happy marriage until her second husband died suddenly of a heart attack in 1975.

She then met Allen Wells, another rock devotee, who regularly visited the shop. 'I said to him, "You're mad if you are also interested in rocks. My first marriage was on the rocks because of rocks." Allen worked with aeroplanes. He was also interested in cacti and railways. He later told me that his first wife couldn't stand railways.'

Allen, Hettie confided, was always a special companion and husband. They respected, and shared, each other's interests, especially a great love for agates. They were together for 20 years.

'Allen was married when I met him. We went on rock-hunting trips together, almost always looking for agates. Then one day Allen was in the shop for a long time. I told him it was time for him to go home. He just looked at me and said, "There is not anything to go home to."'

After 30 years in business selling rocks, Hettie had not become rich but she had made a living. Best of all, she had made a lot of friends. With Allen, she made regular visits to rock shows in Australia and the United

States. She would have liked to have gone to Brazil and collected her own amethyst. But it could only be purchased from the mining companies that laid claim to the amethyst-bearing country. She had some fine examples of amethyst 'pipe' in her shop.

In more recent years the many forms of crystal have become popular for their good vibrations and healing powers. Hettie became an unwilling authority on the mystical qualities of quartz crystals and gemstones when a paper she wrote on the subject was translated and published in Sweden. 'Crystals were always a little alien to me. But thank goodness people still believed in the power of crystals, otherwise I would have had to close my doors,' she once said wryly. Pieces of crystal were frequently purchased for corporate offices. And even if they did not bring the promised results, Hettie said, 'they would still make a beautiful display.'

On one occasion a visitor to Hettie's Rock Shop said, 'There's something here — I can feel very powerful vibrations.' Hettie's

Allen Wells checking out railway wrecks near Arthur's Pass.

nonchalant reply was, 'I have a dinosaur egg.' She then waved an arm towards an unusual shape — about the size of a large ostrich egg — among the disarray of invoice statements and catalogues on her work table. She is believed to have brought the first dinosaur egg into New Zealand. Originating from China's Shandong province, the prized object did not particularly look like an egg.

'How could it after 65 million years?' Hettie retorted. 'It is well and truly fossilised: a piece of ancient rock with impressions suggesting one-time fragments of broken shell. I never expected to see one for sale. I then saw two at Melbourne's Collectors' Corner. I looked and looked and then said, "Why not? A dinosaur egg is not something you see for sale every day!"

'It is really a very ugly thing, but it is a dinosaur egg.'

When Hettie let me hold the precious egg for a few moments I experienced a definite buzz, knowing I was one of a small number of New Zealanders to have had such a Jurassic fragment cupped within my hands.

I am no rockhound, but I always enjoyed my long conversations with Hettie. There was always something new to discuss. And even when she knew she was dying of cancer, she could still encourage and inspire — and make me laugh. I had met her when I was asked to photograph some unusual pieces of Japanese rock art for a local newspaper. Hettie regularly received mail from many countries and she recalled a day in 1971 when she had a letter from Iso Shindo, a rockhound in Japan.

'I didn't know what to do. I couldn't forgive the Japanese for what they did to all those innocent people in Indonesia,' she told me later. But Iso Shindo already knew about Hettie's war experience. He wrote, 'I can understand if you do not want to have anything to do with me, but I was only a boy during the war.'

'I thought about it for a long time,' Hettie said. 'I then realised that we were both admiring the same thing: the beauty in stones.' She met Iso Shindo when he visited New Zealand. He instructed Hettie in suiseki; the Japanese art of stone appreciation. He also sent her some beautiful Japanese Chrysanthemum stones.

But I was continually drawn by Hettie's stories about jade. She was fascinated by the Maori associations with the nephrite greenstone, encouraged a little by Allen's Maori ancestry. She could hold a piece and tell you where it was from, and if it was a good specimen to give to a special friend. She would sort through pieces, saying with authority;

Hettie with her prized fossil dinosaur egg which was excavated in China.

'This is from the Arahura River near Hokitika, and this is from the Taramakau.' Another piece might be from South Westland, or collected from the beach at Barrytown.

The Barrytown piece would be a jade pebble, already partially polished by the flow of the river and by the ocean crashing onto the land. 'The beach pebbles have been washed down the rivers from the mountains. The currents always flow north, taking the jade pieces along the coast and depositing them along the beaches, as far north as Punakaiki, even further.

'When you go looking along the beaches for jade you will see lots of white stones, and lots of coloured stones. Many of them will be green. But when you see greenstone, or jade, you will know straight away what it is.'

She also told me the legends of Chinese jade. The Chinese prefer the lighter coloured stone, known to them for thousands of years as The Stone of Heaven. A piece of jade placed under the tongue of a deceased person guarantees their passage 'to the other side'. But when we talked about the dark green nephrite jade, we were also sharing our love for the South Island, and especially the West Coast. Soon after she arrived in Christchurch Hettie's early rock-hunting excursions took her to the Coast, driving a 'little Standard 10 that always boiled on the top of Porters Pass and Arthur's Pass'. She quickly fell in love with the area, but she had no money to buy the pieces of jade in the shops. 'I would see a piece for 10 shillings, but I never had 10 shillings. That was a lot of money those days.'

In Hokitika she met Theo Schoon, also from Indonesia. A gifted artist who had recently shifted down from the North Island, he became an authority on jade, and jade carving. His popular book, *Jade Country*, weaves a fascinating story about his early unsuccessful attempts to find jade, and on to how he learned to carve the stone.

'Theo got a job carving jade in a Hokitika factory. But he was sacked when he refused to carve a tiki. He would carve anything, but not a tiki. He said the Maoris could carve Maori tikis. He wouldn't carve a pakeha tiki. He got a job cutting scrub along the railway, but his artist hands could not get used to the heavy work, so he was sacked from that job too. He then worked in the hospital looking after mental patients. Then one day he saw himself becoming like them if he stayed much longer.

'Theo just didn't fit in at Hokitika. He asked me to sell his jade in my shop. It took three trips across the mountains in the Standard 10 to carry it all. Once people knew about the jade it sold quickly. Each piece of his jade was unusual.

'He bought an air ticket and went to Sydney. He knew the art world there. He was happy in Sydney, but he didn't do very well. And, by choice, he always lived in derelict places.'

Whenever Hettie visited Sydney rock shows she would visit her friend. She once showed Theo's address to a taxi driver and he said, 'Do you really want to go there?' Hettie replied, 'Yes, a friend of mine lives there.' When they arrived at a block of flats the taxi driver said, 'I will escort you to the door.'

'I knocked at the door. Then a head popped out of an upstairs window and caught my attention. It was Theo. He said, "Hello Hettie, I will drop you down the key and you can come in." I then told the taxi man it was okay for him to go.

'I always brought food for him. He lived on scraps. I would take him to my hotel for a bath, and the bath water would turn black. We would then go to a restaurant for a good meal. We would eat Indonesian or Chinese food.

'He was never appreciated. He taught me to appreciate jade, and that enabled me to become an authority on jade later on.'

She talked a lot about the mystique, or power, of jade. 'It's not a good luck charm. That doesn't really mean anything. It's what you feel. You don't want to part with a special piece of jade. You can't explain what it is. You let people hold it but you always want it back. It can become a protector, and it guides you. A piece of jade can start to mean something to those you give it too.'

Sometime in 1998 Hettie was diagnosed with cancer and given a life expectancy of about two months. It was then she realised that, despite having lived a full and satisfying life in New Zealand's South Island, she was without an identity. 'I feel I don't belong anywhere. I'm a stranger in this country. I have only a son and daughter, and their families, here,' she said ruefully. 'I don't belong to Holland. All my contemporaries have died. I am the last one of my father's line. My father was from an aristocratic family. We all had a title to carry on. When I go that's the finish of it.'

She then related a story about Allen's forefather, an American whaler and boat builder from Massachusetts, who sailed to New Zealand three times during the 1830s; on the third visit he stayed. That was when Ngati Toa chief, Te Rauparaha, was still raiding South Island tribes from his North Island Kapiti base.

'His name was Seth Howland. He became a good friend of Te Rauparaha when he ran two whaling boats from Queen Charlotte Sound, and set up his boat-building at Okains Bay on Banks Peninsula. For

Legends Among the Rocks

services rendered Te Rauparaha gave Allen's ancestor a Maori maiden for a wife. She was high-class girl from Banks Peninsula. Her name was Hari Tiki. She had been taken prisoner by Te Rauparaha in 1830 when she boarded the barque *Elizabeth* in Akaroa Harbour. Unbeknown to her, Te Rauparaha was in cahoots with the infamous Captain John Stewart

Hettie's relative by marriage Seth Howland befriended the famous Maori chief Te Rauparaha.

who concealed some 100 Maori warriors for a surprise revenge attack on the high-ranking Ngai Tahu chief, Te Maiharanui. For a time Hari Tiki became a slave girl at Kapiti.

'Seth Howland and Hari Tiki were married by Bishop Pompallier.

Akaroa, a delightful Banks Peninsula town of French and British origins, was subject to violent raids from the North Island Maori chief, Te Rauparaha.

They had three daughters. One died very early. A second, Phoebe, married a few times and died childless. And a third one, Huldah, married James Wells, who had settled in Okains Bay.'

That is also where Seth Howland is buried although no one is quite sure where. Hari Tiki is believed to have been buried with her people at Port Levy. James and Huldah Wells, and Phoebe, are buried in the Okains Bay cemetery.

Before her death on 1 November 1999, Hettie gifted a large portion of her New Zealand jade collection to the Okains Bay Museum, and she was buried in the nearby cemetery. 'I want to be buried in Okains Bay. I'm a Wells now,' she had said. 'I will be buried close to Wells people. At last I have a feeling of belonging. I feel comfortable.' Hettie had become a South Islander.

CHAPTER 9

PLAYING THE GAME

They would be talking about the Deans episode in Cardiff in 1905. Did he, or did he not, score the try?

John Brooks

In 1952 John Brooks was playing number eight position in the first XV at Hokitika's District High School. One day after a match the coach, Bert O'Brien (who was also his English master) asked, 'John, have you any idea what you want to do when you leave school?'

He replied, 'No Mr O'Brien, I'm enjoying school so much I hadn't thought of leaving.'

The coach then said, 'John, you *are* 18. It's time to move on. 'Have you ever thought of journalism? All the essays you write are in journalese. You're a natural.'

'He put the germ in my mind,' recalls the retired sportswriter almost half a century later. 'Bert O'Brien was our mentor. He coached the cricket team and the rugby team. He was a very interesting man. He always seemed to be so wise, but when he eventually died I worked out that he'd been only 12 years older than us at the time. We depended on him for advice about all sorts of things. Apart from everything else, his death was a tragic loss to the world of laughter.'

Starting on the *Southland Times*, John Brooks moved on to *The Press* where he spent 37 years in the sports department, including six years as sports editor. He accompanied the All Blacks on overseas tours, enjoying a special camaraderie with the players, and he toured with the Canterbury team and many international sides in New Zealand.

'I could write about the players in a way that is difficult to do today,' he says. 'It was almost like a brotherhood, even if you weren't playing with them. You were touring with them, and writing about them. They seemed to respect that.

'I never had to deal through a PR agent as sportswriters do today, and some are quite obstructive I believe. It's a sad commentary on the way the game has gone. Fortunately, my reporting days were all before that happened.'

Rugby tours, especially, had their hilarious moments — there was horse-play, drinking and the occasional punch-up in a hotel — but the

John Brooks with his caricature by The Press *cartoonist Al Nisbet.*

sportswriter and players had a gentleman's agreement. 'You didn't report anything that didn't take place on the field.'

John Brooks has a wry sense of humour, as I discovered when I joined *The Press* in 1987, working in the adjoining department. I had no interest in sport but had willingly spent some Saturday mornings, on request, photographing kids' rugby in North Hagley Park. I had a shot of a promising lad named Andrew Mehrtens, and innocently asked Brooks if this boy had ever gone places in the game. For quite a while he thought I was winding him up. Finally he blurted out, 'Mehrtens? Don't you know he's in the All Black first five?'

But when I started reading stories with the John Brooks byline I was captivated, especially by the personality pieces on almost forgotten sports stars he wrote before his retirement in 1998. Among them were the athlete Valerie Young, yachtsman Peter Mander, who won an Olympic gold medal in Melbourne in 1956, swimming star Tui Shipston, netball's Joan Harnett, speedway champion Ronnie Moore, rugby great Fergie McCormick and many others.

But I was also learning to come to grips with his verbal stories that were as prolific as they were deadpan, consistently told with a seriousness that was finally wrecked by a Brooks grin and a chuckle. There is, for example, the one about the time he represented New Zealand with drinking.

'When the All Blacks toured France in 1977 we had a meal at the big Perpignan winery in south-east France. French television wanted to film an All Black drinking some of the wine of the region. But with a big game next day they said, "No way". So they pushed me forward, and I was given a bottle of fortified wine, something like a port that you don't normally quaff.

'They filmed me drinking, and I had some barbecued snails from a fire made of twigs. They were quite delicious — and I was presented with a tile to commemorate the occasion. I didn't say too much about it at *The Press* at the time.'

John Brooks is a South Islander, born in Christchurch. His father, Tom, was a Magistrate's Court registrar who was transferred to a new centre every two or three years, so John had lived in Napier and Palmerston North before the family relocated to Hokitika in 1950.

'I'd never heard of this place Hokitika. I was unaware people actually

A memento from the 1977 All Black tour of France when, at Perpignan, Brooks was shoved forward to represent New Zealand in drinking!

lived on the West Coast. And when I arrived I thought, blimey — I wondered what I'd struck. I'd arrived from Palmerston North Boys' High where you got caned if you got under 50 per cent in a test. But Hokitika had this easy-ozy atmosphere where the teachers and pupils all seemed to be mates. It took me six months to get used to that sort of atmosphere.'

He talks about sport returning to New Zealand life during the 1950s, having been sidetracked during World War II. 'It was an exciting period for a child watching these great sportsmen playing cricket and rugby. All the great players became part of our everyday lives.'

'Most boys aspired to play rugby. It was so much a part of New Zealand culture, and something in which New Zealand had made a mark in the world doing. In 1924 the All Blacks played 32 games during a tour of Britain and won the lot. They were known as *The Invincibles*.'

He was also inspired by the stories old-timers told when they visited his father. 'They would be talking about the Deans episode in Cardiff in 1905. Did he, or did he not, score the try? Bob Deans was a great South Island player, and grandson of the early Canterbury Deans family. It was the only game the All Blacks lost out of 35 on that British Isles tour.

'Deans had made a run for the line and was tackled. He said he'd forced the ball over the goal line but the referee was back at halfway and hadn't arrived on the scene. He was wearing street shoes, if you please. By the time he got there the Welsh had dragged Deans back and he was actually lying in the field of play. The Welsh claimed he didn't score. The game would have gone to the All Blacks if the try had been awarded and the kick at goal had gone over, as it probably would have.' The Deans episode continued to fascinate him through his sportswriter career.

At the *Southland Times*, when John Brooks started in 1953, even junior reporters were expected to cover sport. 'But I was told I would be put into the reading room for 12 months to learn the style. I was then promised the subs' bench for 12 months. And if they then thought I had a future as a reporter, I would be turned loose. I was horrified.'

He soon had a lucky break when three reporters were fired within two months.

'One got drunk and didn't cover a meeting he was supposed to. The second was assigned to cover an athletics meeting one Saturday. But he was mad on racing, so he went to the Riverton Races. Unfortunately the chief reporter was also at the race meeting and spied him.

'The third played a trick on the chief sub — he said there was a murder story one night. The chief sub got very excited because nothing ever happened in Invercargill in those days. When a cat got run over, that was news. He kept the chief sub on tenterhooks for an hour and gleefully acknowledged it was a hoax. And he got fired for that.

'So all of a sudden I was plucked from the reading room and made into a reporter. I became number three rugby reporter which delighted me. But they also gave me swimming and, in a sense, they threw me into the deep end.'

He recalls a career blunder soon after starting in the sports department at *The Press* in 1961. He was deputy to sports editor Dick Brittenden who, apart from his brilliant sports writing, principally on cricket, churned out more than 5000 of the Christchurch paper's pithy 'Random Reminder' features.

'By that stage I was covering club rugby which was okay because the All Blacks played club rugby in those days. But I didn't expect to be assigned to a school game. So when I looked in the assignment book and saw my name beside the Christ's College vs Boys' High School I asked, "Is this a mistake, Dick?"

'"No no," he said. "I want you to go and report it."

'I said, "But I have done test matches — this is a school game!"

R.T. (Dick) Brittenden *was sports editor when John Brooks joined* The Press *in 1961. (Photograph* The Press*)*

'He looked at me with horror. He then said, "This is *the* game."

'I had a rude awakening. When I went to the Christ's College ground the Mayor of Christchurch George Manning was there with his robes and gold chain, Lady Manning, Bob McFarlane, the former mayor, and MP for Christchurch Central, other MPs, Bishops of Christchurch — Catholic and Anglican — and Sir John and Lady Ormond from Hawke's Bay.

'With such a distinguished gallery I realised this school game had a certain status. But I was just a dumb bastard from Southland. How was I to know that a Christ's College vs Boys' High game rated higher than a test match?'

Another blunder followed back at *The Press* after the game. A Ranfurly Shield match was being played in some other part of New Zealand that day. 'I had a visit by the editor Rolle Cant asking, "What was the result of the big game today?"

'I said, "I don't know, Mr Cant, our wireless is broken and we haven't got the results through yet."

'He said, "No, the school game!"

'The score was something like 11–9 to Boys' High School. Cant and Brittenden were both Boys' High old boys.'

In those days *The Press* employed Green & Hahn on contract to do all the newspaper's photography and John Brooks recalls Morrie Calvert who was known as 'One-shot Morrie': he went on an assignment and took one picture, and that was it.

'If you didn't like it, it was hard luck. He took one picture of that game and for those days it was superb. The Boys' High captain, Don Johnston, got his head cut open with a sprig. He went off and got it stitched and a big bandage was put on his head. He came back on. About two minutes to go, Johnston scored the winning try. He came running out of the mist, heading for goal line. Morrie was there, right on the spot.'

He recalls a more austere *Press* in the 1960s. 'They had standards that were maintained rigidly. The subs bench was a sort of Who's Who of the great brains of Canterbury. Ted Glasgow was chief sub. Lewis Fitch, his deputy, looked like someone out of a Hemingway novel. He smoked a pipe and he had a big blue pencil for tightening up the copy. They had the ability to take down anyone who was up themselves, but they always had very sound advice. The whole time the reporters were being stimulated.'

For many years John enjoyed a love-hate relationship with the Canterbury player and All Black (and one-time coach of both) Alex (Grizz) Wyllie. 'The uncrowned King of Omihi in North Canterbury, Grizz was a hard man. He played his rugby hard. Played hard off the field. He was always a fair bloke as well.

'Every morning during a four-month tour of North America and Britain in 1972 and 1973 we met in the foyer. He would be going out to training, "Well, Brooks," he'd say in his jocular manner, "what shit are you writing today?" It got a bit monotonous, like a tap dripping.'

In Wales, Brooks was attempting to work in a Newport hotel room with no central light. As the agent for The Press Association, he had to write eight or 10 stories a day for a raft of morning and evening papers. 'Not only did this particular bedroom have no central light, the one bedside lamp had a weak 25-watt bulb. In the toilet en suite, however, there was a very bright light. But it was way up high. I couldn't reach to

Alex (Grizz) Wyllie, the Canterbury rugby coach at Lancaster Park (now Jade Stadium) in 1985. Brooks and Grizz had their differences. (courtesy The Press)

take it out. I did the simple thing: I lowered the toilet seat and put the portable typewriter on it. I found a wee chair and sat with my knees up round my face. I was typing away when Grizz came into my room and stood over me. I looked up and he said, "Well Brooks, at last you've found surroundings to fit what you write."

Then, in 1983, Brooks won a national Sportswriter of the Year award, at a time when the print media was pitted against radio and television commentators and photographers. Later the Canterbury Rugby Supporters' Club decided to salute his achievement by presenting him with a set of inscribed goblets at its annual dinner, and Canterbury captain Don Hayes was selected to do the honours. 'I hear you've won some sort of award,' he said during pre-dinner drinks. 'How did you get it — in a raffle?'

Churning out sports results every day in *The Press* building was the downside of the job. Once John started touring with international teams, he was meeting legends of rugby and finding out what actually happened at a particular game. He recalls his first trip overseas, and the adrenaline pumping as he looked down on New York from an aircraft loaded with All Blacks. Then there was the excitement of writing and filing stories back to New Zealand.

He also saw opportunities to fine-tune his writing, especially under extreme deadlines. He would take his stories down to the nearest telegraph branch at the post office where an operator punched them out on a tape.

'You filled in a form a bit like the old telegram form. Each paper had a code. You wrote "Press Collect" and signed your name. Mike Robson, who was later to become managing director of INL, was the NZPA Bureau chief in London. He rang one day when I was in Dublin.

'"PA is very unhappy with you," he said. "You filed a couple of stories yesterday. One ended up in Ecuador and the other was in Johannesburg."

'He asked how it had happened. I said, "I don't know." I'd been sending the stories the same way for months. Mike Robson told me to go around to the post office and ask to see the supervisor, and give them a rark-up.

'I met a charming man. He offered me a cup of tea, and even a whisky. I told him that PA was very unhappy.

'"It's not us," he said with an accent as broad as a plank. "It's the English. They don't like us you see. All the stories from us have to go through London. When they see a story from Dublin they pigeon-hole it for three or four hours, and then they send it to another destination just to stuff us up."

Overseas trips also enabled John Brooks to pick up tenuous threads of the Deans story. At home he had interviewed Bob Deans's brother, Douglas, when he was in his 80s. 'He just said he could not say yea or nay but "if Bob said he scored, then he scored."' In 1972 he went out to a small village near Cardiff and interviewed the last survivor of that game. He was Willy Llewellyn, the Welsh wing three-quarter. 'Aged 96 his memory was reasonably good. But if he got off the point I didn't like to push him. In the end I asked, "Do you think Deans got the try?"

'He sighed and eventually he said, "Well I don't know. I was on the ground at the time. I'd just tackled Billy Wallace who'd passed to Deans. I couldn't see from where I was, but it was a good movement. It deserved to end in a try."

'I said. "That'll do me." Wales had scored the only try of the match. Then he said, "But Wales had three other chances to score. Each time there was only the fullback from New Zealand to beat. But each time, alas, the man with the ball wanted all the glory for himself but not for Wales."

'In a sense that was the end of the matter. As a boy I'd heard of the great injustice done to New Zealand during that 1905 game. In actual fact it would have been an injustice to Wales had they been beaten. Wales was the better team on the day.'

It was on the 1972 tour, too, that Otago prop forward Keith Murdoch was sent home in disgrace following a punch-up with a security guard in Cardiff's Angel Hotel. Brooks called PA and told them to hold the morning papers until he could dictate the story. 'As it happened, that was also the night *The Press* published the university examination results. Students were crowding Press Lane to await the first edition. But when the paper was late owing to the Murdoch story there was almost another riot in Christchurch.'

In 1992 he wrote a story, 'Exit the wild man', telling how Murdoch had been set up and provoked by an obnoxious Welsh security guard who, it is believed, was dismissed from his job some years later. In shame Murdoch disappeared into Australia, moving from job to job and living in a self-imposed exile. John Brooks says Murdoch had a lot of support from his team-mates, and especially fellow test prop Jeff Matheson who thought Murdoch was cast as a villain by the British media. 'It was almost

Demi Sakata playing for All Japan in Wellington. He was a prolific scorer of tries. (courtesy The Press)

as if they were trying to get rid of him,' he said when interviewed 20 years after the event. 'But I'll tell you this — if Keith returned to Dunedin tomorrow he'd get a hero's welcome.'

Back home John Brooks gathered a stack of newspaper clippings preserving the stories of famous, and unusual, sportspeople. He interviewed Yoshihiro Sakata, the fast Japanese wing three-quarters who played for Canterbury during the 1960s. 'He came here with the All-Japan side and scored five tries against New Zealand Juniors in 1968. He played for a season with the university side, scoring 18 tries, which was a record for Christchurch at that stage. He returned to New Zealand for two or three more seasons, ending up being included in the Five Players of the Year chosen by the *Rugby Almanac of New Zealand*.

'He was a popular player and very good with an impressive tally of 47 tries in 39 matches while playing in Christchurch. His team mates called him "Yoshikiwi" because he integrated very easily. He also had the nickname Demi (big eyes). In his own country where Demi played for the Kinko Railway team, he was regarded as an expert in the noble art of scoring tries.'

John says sportspeople were 'always blatantly honest in retrospect'. They did not seek glory for themselves. If they had done something shady for the sake of the team, they would own up. And they were always quite chuffed that you wanted to write about them.

'As an interviewer, I always let people have their say. Often they'd tell me I'd said the right thing. They appreciated that because they didn't quite know how to express it all themselves.'

'But the most important advice I received was from a veteran journo, "Jop" Watt, at the start of my career. "Never betray a confidence," he said. "You might get one good story by doing that, but that'll be the last one you get from that source."'

South

CHAPTER 10

ARTIST IN THE MOUNTAINS

> *I used to enjoy drawing as a child. I was no better than anyone else, but one day I found I could represent the mountains reasonably well.*
>
> Austen Deans

If he had followed his family tradition, Austen Deans would have become a farmer on the Malvern Hills near Darfield. But he was not cut out for farming. What did interest him was the wonderful landscape, and particularly the mountains around his home. Growing up, he would follow the ridges with his eye to see where they went, looking for ways to the summit. He would watch the changing patterns of light, and how light and shadow described the shape and form of a landscape.

'I got my inspiration from the mountains,' he says. 'I used to enjoy drawing as a child. I was no better than anyone else, but one day I found I could represent the mountains reasonably well.'

These days, aged in his mid-80s and living among podocarp forest close under Canterbury's Mount Peel, he will modestly tell you that he is still representing the mountains 'reasonably well'. In his wonderfully cluttered home you can see a collection of huge dramatic canvases in oils — and smaller delicate watercolours — depicting the South Island alpine landscapes that have dominated his life. And works signed A.A. Deans are well represented in homes and galleries throughout the South Island and New Zealand. Many have gone overseas, and the whereabouts of some — produced when he was a prisoner of war in Europe — remain a mystery. But the reasons for his art remain unpretentious: he simply wants to bring something back to remind him of his ventures into the bush and the mountains.

'I enjoy being out among the mountains, and art has been a means to exist. I can't tell you why I love mountains. They just thrill me. I can't help it. I've had a job that has been completely compatible with my wishes — possibly because I paint things that appeal to lot of people, especially in Canterbury. I've been enormously lucky.'

By his own admission, his ability shows no signs of slipping, and nor does his output. He had no time for an interview during the winter when he seizes every opportunity to paint in the low light. When he is not painting, he is working with his wife Liz and willing family helpers, returning their 40-hectare hillside block to native bush. Even when I did get him to stop, he was working on a forthcoming exhibition in Geraldine.

Austen Deans wanted to become a self-supporting artist during the 1930s when only about three New Zealand artists were earning their entire income from their painting. Most were teaching, and using their art to supplement their regular income. 'Sydney Thompson was the most successful self-supporting artist and, in my opinion, one of our greatest

Austen Deans working in his Peel Forest studio. (November 2000)

Detail from a watercolour depicting Little Mount Peel, overlooking Peel Forest in South Canterbury.

painters,' Austen says. 'He was born in Oxford, a small Canterbury town, but he always said he was an "Oxford man".'

Austen got a great deal of help from the family farm, despite the fact that there were no artists among his ancestors. One of Canterbury's pioneering families, the Deans were farming stock. They produced a famous rugby player, Bob Deans, who toured the British Isles with the All Blacks in 1905, but an artist in the family was a new experience.

After leaving Christ's College Austen spent five years at the Canterbury College School of Art, and then eight months as a farmer-artist until the Second World War began. 'Whenever there wasn't much farm work I'd go off on a painting trip. That way, my art was kept alive.'

His ambition was to go London's Slade School of Art which shaped many of New Zealand's major painters, including Olivia Spencer Bower and Peter McIntyre. But the war intervened. 'I joined up despite being a pacifist in my thoughts. But I knew that Nazism was something that had to be met head on. Frank Shurrock, our sculpture teacher, had influenced me in pacifism, and he joined up as well.

'I was promoted to lance-corporal two weeks after the start of war, and was still a lance-corporal at the end. I think I was the longest serving lance-corporal in the whole British forces,' he laughs. 'I was never promoted, but I never lost what I had, even though I deserved to once or twice.'

But he was taken prisoner by the Germans, spending nine months in hospital in Greece, 18 months in Poland, three months near Berlin and the last 18 months in Austria. 'Travelling between these places I got to see quite a lot of Europe from the wrong side of the wire.'

In Greece he managed to get himself an excellent watercolour set — by devious means. He painted a lot of people with interesting faces, especially in Greece and Poland, and a self-portrait that was later to inspire artists in New Zealand. 'We had to work hard during the day, but we had long evenings. Art helped to keep my sanity. The officers who were prisoners were not allowed to work. When I met them after the war I discovered many of them had gone loopy. The exception was Charlie Upham from North Canterbury. He spent his time planning elaborate escapes.'

Austen's only attempt at escape, in Austria, ended with three weeks in a civilian jail. Using a pair of pliers, he made an unobtrusive hole in the wire and at night, undetected, he would explore the hills and raid local vegetable gardens. Surprisingly, his thefts never attracted any complaints. 'People must have noticed when they went out one morning and found all their pumpkins had suddenly disappeared.' One night he and a few others escaped, it snowed when, he says, it shouldn't have. 'Our tracks were easy to follow and when the Germans started shooting at us we saw no point in it,' he recalls wryly.

With help from the Red Cross he managed to get about 130 of his drawings and paintings through to Britain, but the bulk of them were left behind in a trunk addressed to the Red Cross. 'I had to just leave it behind when we were marched out ahead of the advancing British troops. Some time later an Austrian ski instructor who was working at Mount Cook returned to the village but he couldn't find any trace. There were one or two I regret not having.'

Marriage in 1947 to Liz (Elizabeth Hutton) from the neighbouring farm helped to return him to normal after the war, or as he says, 'as normal as I've been able. But I think I've always been a bit different.'

After the war he was also able to get a bursary for study overseas but it would not pay for the hoped-for five-year course at the Slade. Instead he spent two years at the much smaller Sir John Cass College. 'It was like a small university with a strong art school and a school of navigation. Cass was a good experience but more from the philosophy side of art. During my time as a prisoner of war I had met two Australian artists whose drawing ability was far and away ahead of my own. They were into modernism. I thought there must be something in it because the Australians were dissatisfied with art as we knew it.

'I did my best to get into it but it didn't mean anything to me. In the end I came to the conclusion it was all a matter of fashion. I'm not interested in fashion at all. A lecture at the Cass confirmed me in this.'

He says he is not an artist with a capital 'A' and he tried hard to join the so-called 'real art' people. 'Maybe my make-up was just too simple. Artists like Billy Sutton were intellectual. He was an artist who did all sorts of styles very successfully. I loved to see the art but had no concern to do it myself.'

And Austen says he might have made much better money if he had carried on with the portrait side of art. But he wanted to be out in the hills, not in a studio stewing over someone's portrait.

During the 1930s Austen Deans had met the delightfully crusty Duncan Darroch, who lived in the famous little artist's cottage near The Hermitage hotel in Mount Cook Village. Darroch had arrived in New Zealand as a sailor from the island of Jura in the north of Scotland.

'He had a real feel for the mountains and he painted them beautifully, often using the pointillism technique where spots of vibrant colour side by side produce a blended effect to capture the light. 'Too many artists draw mountains as a backdrop. You look at them and think that if you fell off, you'd slide gently to the bottom. Darroch's mountains looked dangerous. If you fell off one of his mountains, you'd hurt yourself.

'I hadn't been painting long when I first met him. He saw a bit of a sketch I was doing and told me to carry on. He was painting the things I wanted to paint.'

Later Austen heard a tragic love story involving Darroch. After he had been in New Zealand for three or four years he was diagnosed with TB and it was suggested he that went to live where the mountain air might do him some good.

'I understand that he had met a girl in New Zealand and broke off the relationship because he didn't believe if would be fair to marry her after he was diagnosed with TB with, perhaps, only a few years to live. As it turned out, about two years later when he visited the specialist, it was confirmed the diagnosis had been wrong. He was in fact suffering from something else that, whatever it was, had cured itself. In the meantime his girl had gone overseas and was never traced.'

Austen Deans also learned a lot from veteran mountaineer and Fiordland pioneer Edgar Williams who enjoyed the mountains almost until he died in 1983, aged 91. Williams, who had been photographing the Fiordland Peaks as early as 1917, turned up at the School of Art and suggested he and Austen went out on a trip somewhere. 'He wanted a companion and he knew that as a self-employed artist I could pick up my pack whenever it suited Edgar.' But it was not until after the war

Veteran mountaineer Edgar Williams found his way through Fiordland's mountains.

when they went out together and, in 1955, made the first ascent of the Llawrenny Peaks (1932 metres) in Fiordland.

'I learned a lot from Edgar. He had a wonderful attitude towards things, particularly when we got into Fiordland. I had no idea how to get from A to B in that sort of terrain but he just said, "we will go this way" and we went a way I wouldn't have thought possible — Fiordland must have more vertical land than horizontal.

'Edgar had an objective to reach the peak, but a second objective was to enjoy every step of the way. He didn't ever hurry. He gradually got even slower, partly through getting older but partly through enjoying being in the bush, on the tussock, or climbing on rock.

'The Llawrenny Peaks was one of Edgar's real ambitions. You can just see part of them, looking up Sinbad Gully beside Mitre Peak.'

Austen Deans and Edgar Williams were joined by Ray Copp and Marty Bassett. 'The peaks were very difficult to get at, but Edgar found a way. To my knowledge they've not been climbed since. Not so long ago Marty Bassett went for a flight over the Llawrenny Peaks. He said the glaciers we saw have nearly all gone. The whole mountain is quite different.'

Austen recalls younger climbers criticising Edgar Williams because he often bivvied out on the mountains. If they got caught out they said they were doing an 'Edgar Williams'. But in Williams's case it was quite deliberate: 'Other climbers were faster and loved to get back to a comfortable tent. Edgar said you don't really feel part of mountains until you've bivvied out without a tent. In his younger days he had to cycle to the mountains.

'I was fond of the old boy. He was a lot older than me, but he almost seemed to be everlasting. He never looked old. He never was old. He was always still learning.'

Austen Deans talks about the South Island's different mountain regions. He has a special affinity for the Rangitata River valley close to his Mount Peel home. He enjoys the remoteness of the Rangitata, and the mystique bestowed by Samuel Butler. 'The river is rather different in that the Rangitata starts where two other large rivers meet; the Clyde and the Havelock.'

Climbing, and painting Mount D'Archiac have also been special experiences. But he also enjoys the different flavour of the Rakaia and Waimakariri valleys further north. Then Mount Cook and the Waitaki

Detail from Llawrenny Peaks, one of the most isolated of Fiordland's mountains, painted by Austen Deans in 1956. He was in the party that made the first ascent the year before.

valley is different again. 'Samuel Butler made a statement about Mount Cook which was quite wonderful. He said, "If a person says *he thinks* he has seen Mount Cook, you can be quite sure that he hasn't seen it. The moment it comes into sight the exclamation is 'That's Mount Cook' — not 'That *must* be Mount Cook!' There is no possibility of mistake."'

Austen Deans says Cook is a wonderful block of mountain, but he did not particularly enjoy climbing it. His friend Limbo Thompson took him and Gerald Nanson to the summit in 1972. With them was Philip Osborne who was killed soon after while climbing Cook's Caroline Face. 'I did it just to say I have. But it wasn't really the mountains for me. There were sightseeing planes flying over the whole time. I love to be in the mountains, and believe I'm the only person there for miles.'

On many of his tramping and climbing ventures he has worn a kilt. It is less a reflection of his Scottish family heritage — who were lowlanders anyway — than the sheer practicability of the garment which is 'very nice to walk in with no drag at the knees and surprisingly warm when you needed it'.

He has always loved Peel Forest. 'It's like a little bit Westland but having the advantage of a better Canterbury climate. As a child I always stood in awe of the bush. There's something very ancient and awe-inspiring about the New Zealand bush. The native forests are thought

An impressive stand of Podocarp forest close to the artist's home.

to be remnants of the bush that covered the earth in the time of the dinosaurs. 'I still feel sensitive to the atmosphere of the bush.'

The conversation returns to Austen's art. He says he is better with watercolour than oils, and he talks about the differences between photography and painting. 'The camera leaves nothing to the imagination unless it is used by a photographer who is a real artist, able to focus on one object and let a lot go vague. The painter subsists on indicating rather than fully stating. A tremendous lot of detail is left out and represented by a plain wash. Minimal painters take that idea to the extreme, but it's amazing what they can indicate with very few strokes on a huge canvas.

'If possible I like to work in the outdoors. There's inspiration out there. I can take elements directly out of a large piece of countryside. If you work from a photograph, it's all cut out for you and the painting risks becoming dry and artificial. To me the mountains are all characters. Each area has its character — I like to capture that character and I can understand how each mountain came to look the way it does.'

His painting, he claims, has changed little over the years. Even so they are continually displayed and catalogued with some big price tags. He does wonder, however, how his art would have been without the war. 'If I could have carried on from art school in Christchurch to the Slade, I suspect I might I have been better. My training would have been more thorough during my formative years. But the war may have done more for my character. I don't know.'

The question will remain unanswered. But it is certain that the South Island mountains Austen Deans paint are dangerous. You would not want to fall off one of them; they are real. His art tells you he is a true man of the mountains.

CHAPTER 11
CHOWBOK OF EREWHON

> *You found a better thing than 'country' —*
> *you found Erewhon.*
> From a letter to Samuel Butler
> by a fellow runholder

When Samuel Butler's famous satire *Erewhon* was published in 1872, some of the finest descriptions of the South Island's Southern Alps were preserved in literature. For about three years during the 1860s Butler, an Englishman, had a sheep run known as Mesopotamia, situated in a desolate area beneath the rugged mountains overlooking the upper reaches of the Rangitata River. He was an artist and an accomplished musician as well as a writer. And he made some remarkable exploratory journeys in the mountains.

Butler's 'Erewhon' — the title is simply 'nowhere' spelt backwards, well, almost — bestowed considerable mystique on the remote Rangitata region. He wrote the book in England, half a world away:

> *I am there now as I write; I fancy that I can see the downs, the huts, the plain, and the riverbed — that torrent pathway of desolation, with its distant roar of waters. Oh, wonderful! Wonderful! So lonely and so solemn, with the sad grey clouds above and no sound save a lost lamb bleating upon the mountain-side, as though its little heart were breaking . . .*

Butler's descriptions of the South Island alpine landscape in the opening chapters of *Erewhon* chapters captured my attention many years ago but my curiosity was soon directed to the fictional characters Mr Biggs, and especially his reluctant companion Chowbok, described, somewhat unkindly, as 'stupid and grotesquely ugly'. Together, Biggs and Chowbok set out to find a way over the mountains from inland Canterbury to what we know as the South Island West Coast. Chowbok is a sort of chief among natives and a great favourite of the missionaries.

The road to Erewhon, and the Erewhon mountains, seen from above Potts Cutting. Early in the nineteenth century wool wagoner, Chas Dunstan, wrote of the scene: 'I have been in many lands and I cannot get interested in old Abbeys or Pyramids. Cities are just so much bricks and mortar and concrete canyons, but I still think that the view from the top of Potts Cutting, to be the most inspiring and uplifting sight, that I have ever seen.'

He speaks little English and does little work. His main aim is to get rum from the shearers, and he becomes dangerous when drunk. Biggs is nevertheless pleased to have Chowbok as a travelling companion. Besides, he has a great ambition to convert him to Christianity, and even goes so far as to baptise him.

At first Biggs and Chowbok have an easy journey on horseback up a wide riverbed, but they then have to negotiate a narrow precipitous gorge where it takes them two hours to cover less than a mile. Eventually they come to a saddle and then a riverbed that opens out wide above the gorge. At last they can see the main range where 'the glaciers were tumbling down the mountain-sides like cataracts, and seemed actually to descend upon the riverbed'. Owing to some ancient tribal belief, Chowbok has a great fear of the higher mountains. When his master approaches too close, he takes flight and returns as hard as he can go to the less hostile river valley.

Left to his own devices, Biggs ascends a saddle that is now known as Butler's Saddle, a high mountain pass between the Lawrence and Rakaia Rivers. From this splendid vantage point he discovers a way through the mountains, via the Whitcombe Pass. It is beyond these mountains where he has his strange Erewhonian adventures, in a country where machines are banned, sick people are imprisoned as criminals and criminals are cared for as though they were sick. But who was Butler's model for the strange character Chowbok?

His real name was Andy Bittern, a fleet-footed Australian Aboriginal whose life ended tragically on a British gallows in Western Australia. Andy, who originally came from the Swan River in Western Australia, is thought to have arrived in New Zealand as a servant of Sir George Grey when he became governor of the colony in 1845. During the late 1850s Andy was working as a mail carrier, running the 160 kilometres between Christchurch and Timaru.

Mesopotamia in the 1860s, from a watercolour by William Packe. Samuel Butler's cottage is on the right.

Chowbok of Erewhon

The mark of Andy Bittern, made on 28 April 1860, when he agreed to work for Acland and Tripp for £25 a year. Andy, who could not read or write, would have been unaware his name was spelt wrongly. (from the Mount Peel diaries.)

Andy then became a servant at Mount Peel Station, the large sheep run in South Canterbury then jointly owned by two young men, John Acland and Charles Tripp. In 1858 Charles Tripp married Ellen, a daughter of Henry Harper, the first Anglican Bishop of Christchurch. And it is from Ellen Tripp's writings that we have some first-hand information about Andy Bittern, who was also known as 'Handy Andy', owing to his ingenious methods of repairing huts and fences, and 'Black Andy'. His fictional name 'Chowbok' may have meant 'cowboy'.

Although he had almost no book learning, Andy nevertheless possessed some extraordinary abilities. As well as being a very good runner, he was an excellent tracker. On a wet, cold day, a visitor arriving at Mount Peel from Ashburton discovered, to his horror, that he had lost an important letter on the way. Andy said, 'Me find letter,' and set out to swim the Rangitata and cross the trackless Canterbury Plains. He found the letter near Hinds and, within four hours of starting, was back at Mount Peel, having completed a round trip of some 55 kilometres.

On another occasion Charles Tripp had a letter he wanted delivered in Christchurch. The rivers were in flood and considered uncrossable by most of the men but, undaunted, Andy started running at first light. He swam the roaring Rangitata, Ashburton and Rakaia Rivers and arrived in Christchurch by nightfall. It was a remarkable feat, since it took a good rider a full day to cover the 130 kilometres between Mount Peel and Christchurch. Andy's next known run was in March 1861, when

Ellen Tripp photographed in 1901. From her writings we have first-hand information about the young Australian Aboriginal Andy Bittern.

he ran all the way to Christchurch just to see Ellen Tripp's newly born daughter; such was his devotion to the family he served.

Andy Bittern's feats impressed a famous New Zealand runner, Don Cameron, who made numerous long-distance runs in New Zealand and Australia — including Sydney to Melbourne — during the 1970s and 1980s. 'Andy Bittern's running feats were outstanding, especially without the benefits of modern equipment and training. Furthermore, in the 1860s, he would have been running over rough, tussocky, almost roadless ground. And what would he have had on his feet?'

Regrettably, Andy had a failing that eventually led to his downfall. As mail carrier he had developed a liking for rum and he always asked for a glass at the end of a journey. Most people were only too pleased to oblige because Andy never asked for any other payment. But, like the fictional Chowbok, Andy became a madman when he had had too much to drink. He was at odds with the police so often that he eventually developed the habit of running to the police station at the completion of a journey. There, he would be safely locked up until he was ready to leave next morning.

In spite of Andy's drinking problem, Ellen Tripp had complete confidence in the children's safety when they were with him. He would make them toys, and take them away among the forest and hills for hours at a time. He had a special affinity for the Tripps' first child, Howard, who held Andy in high regard.

After Samuel Butler took up his sheep run at Mesopotamia in 1860, he became a constant visitor at Mount Peel. He was an excellent pianist and spent many hours at the Tripps' piano 'which was a delightful treat so far away from any pleasures of that kind'. Charles Tripp enjoyed

The Mount Peel Station buildings where Andy Bittern lived.

debating with Butler, but Ellen was not so sure about his wild theories, many of which were later incorporated into *Erewhon*. 'His was a peculiar nature,' she wrote.

There is little doubt that Samuel Butler would have met Andy at Mount Peel and may have invited him to Mesopotamia, which, for Andy, was a short 50 kilometre jog up the south bank of the Rangitata River. It seems likely that Butler took Andy exploring among the wild mountains and, in this environment, so vastly different from the flatness of Western Australia, the character Chowbok was born.

Some time in 1862, Andy Bittern was sent back to Australia after he had threatened to kill Charles Tripp for refusing to give him more rum. His expulsion must have been a blow to Andy and to those whom he had served so well, but it seemed there was no alternative because the Tripps did not want to see him locked up. Andy returned to his tribe at the Swan River and shortly after met a tragic end. Acting in accordance with his tribal law, he killed a man who had murdered his mother and was hanged by the British. His friends at Mount Peel were upset when

The Mount Peel homestead of today, still lived in by descendants of John Acland.

they eventually heard of these events, believing the sentence to be unduly harsh considering the great provocation.

As Chowbok, Andy lives on in literature. But if the author of *Erewhon* did not give him all the credit he deserved, he has a finer memorial among the splendid mountains of South Canterbury. In 1933 a party of Canterbury mountaineers was attempting to cross Butler's Saddle enroute to the Rakaia River. In error they went too far up the Lawrence River and climbed onto a high col to the east of Butler's Saddle. Realising their mistake, the climbers decided to perpetuate the name of Biggs's companion in *Erewhon* and in 1945 the name Chowbok Col was officially approved.

More than a century after Samuel Butler and Andy Bittern left the Rangitata, mystery still surrounds the tall mountains: 'You found a better thing than "country" — you found Erewhon,' a fellow runholder once wrote to Butler. Although it feels remote, the region is reasonably accessible from Christchurch. A shingle road heading inland from Mount Somers ends at the historic sheep station, Erewhon, under the mountains at the source of the mighty Rangitata. Across the wide riverbed is Mesopotamia, where some relics of Butler's time remain. And Mount Peel station, near the popular Peel Forest Park, is still owned by descendants of John Acland, the original runholder. And the evidence that a remarkable young Australian Aboriginal once lived there is confined to a few entries in the early Mount Peel diaries.

CHAPTER 12

BACK COUNTRY BARD

We were often referred to as the great boozers, but in those days a musterer carried only two bottles of beer simply because there was no room for more.
Ross McMillan

I am attracted to unsung heroes, and small South Island towns are full of them. Take, for example, a Naseby sheep farmer and poet I met for the first time in 1984. Ross McMillan was writing under the pen name 'Blue Jeans' — and he still is. It is easy to warm to this back-country bard whose haunting homespun verse has captured *Central Otago News* readers for more than two decades.

'Blue Jeans' is best described as a sort of New Zealand Henry Lawson with a little of Tennyson dropped in, along with a wee bit of Robert Burns for good measure. His ballads weave a nostalgic story of Central Otago, expressing a deep passion for Central's mountains. They recall the gold rushes and the stockmen, shepherds and shearers who followed, along with the musterers who roamed the hills on horseback. And that strange Scottish game, curling, played every winter on Central Otago's frozen lakes, is also lovingly preserved in rhyming lines. 'Blue Jeans' writes with deep feeling about the people of Central, their tragedies, humour, weaknesses and strengths, yet he is still to find a wider (and deserved) recognition in New Zealand literature.

He had written about 500 pieces when I caught up with him again early in 2000. 'Yes, I still write a few. Not as many as I used to,' he told me in his southern burr. 'I'm in my 70s now, and a great-granddad to a bunch of red-haired kids. But I still have a horse and five dogs. And every year I ride in the four-day Otago Goldfields Cavalcade, along the heritage tracks our forebears rode. I'm very happy with my lot.'

Ross McMillan in 1984. He is still weaving a nostalgic story of Central Otago through his Blue Jeans ballads.

Ross McMillan, born in Central Otago, left school in 1945 to become a horse breaker. Over the years he worked as a musterer, shearer and rouseabout on most Central Otago high-country stations before taking over his parents' Naseby sheep farm in partnership with his brother. His experiences as a rouseabout, or 'rousie', have provided a background for much of his literary work:

> *A rousie or rouse-a-bout,*
> *My home is anywhere.*
> *Along the tracks, a down and out,*
> *Where there are sheep to shear.*

I travel with a memory,
That never seems to shrink.
And when my dreams catch up with me,
I drown them in drink.

He married, had two children Peter and Jane, and then in 1982 his wife Rae died. She had suffered from multiple sclerosis for about 15 years and during that time he had run his farm and organised the children. He was usually up early and out on the tractor before returning home to get his son and daughter ready for school. In the little spare time he had, he started writing his verse 'in an effort to stay sane'. Looking back on those years, he still wears an expression of bewilderment. 'I married a healthy country girl, had two sound children, then spent many of my youthful years playing the role of a nurse.' These difficult years may help to explain why the poetry of 'Blue Jeans' reflects so much regret mixed with nostalgia.

He wrote his first poem in 1960 while on holiday in the North Island, and feeling homesick for his Central Otago mountains. 'Way Le' Go' is the story of a mother waiting by the stockyard for her overdue son who has gone out on a thoroughbred mare that is 'halfbroken and wild with

Once a common sight in rural New Zealand. Ross McMillan laments the passing of the working farm horse.

the hatred of man . . .' The horse and the boy have gone over a cliff, and the dogs watch and wait, not knowing why their master is lying so still.

'Way Le' Go', which bears some similarity to Banjo Paterson's 'Lost', was originally thought out while droving sheep through Dansey's Pass from North Otago to the Maniototo. Ross recalls finishing eight verses and wondering how to sign himself. 'I then saw a Maori kid wearing blue jeans, an attire that was not so common then as it is now.' Taken by the sight, he signed himself 'Blue Jeans' and sent his first effort off to the *Auckland Weekly News*. To his surprise, a few weeks later he received a cheque.

Most of his subsequent work has been published in the *Central Otago News*, for which he would write a piece every week. 'You would see something in print and that gave you the encouragement to write another,' he says. Every so often the paper would publish several 'Blue Jeans' poems in a small, but attractive, collection. Some of his poems have also been put to music by New Zealand folk singer Phil Garland, whose favourite, 'Down a Country Road I Know', became the title track of a solo album:

> *There are shearing sheds I shore in that are scattered by the way,*
> *And I seem to hear the clatter of the cutters making play*
> *And the laughter of the shearers from the days of long ago,*
> *When they called me 'Jim the Ringer' down a country road I know.*

Ross McMillan showed no inclination to write verse when he was at school, although he admits to being impressed by the works of Banjo Paterson and Henry Lawson, the two Australians he claims were 'the greatest writers'. During a visit to Australia 40 years ago he realised that all the things Banjo Paterson wrote about existed in New Zealand.

Some of the best of 'Blue Jeans' undoubtedly recalls the musterers, shearers and horses before they were replaced in the high country by four-wheel drive tracks and helicopters. 'We were often referred to as the great boozers, but in those days a musterer carried only two bottles of beer simply because there was no room for more. Musterers these days buy canned beer in more convenient packs and have them carried in a four-wheel drive. Sometimes, in a mountain hut, you'll even find a cook.'

In isolated shearing sheds Ross discovered where the stories were told, and where much of the South Island high-country folklore originated. He talks fondly about the last of the mule trains on Central Otago's Kyeburn and Mount Ida stations and builds an image in verse of those little long-eared animals, threading their way up through rocks and scree high on the mountains every spring and autumn. 'They were hardy creatures that could carry incredibly heavy loads. They won the affection and admiration from all the men out on the hills.'

Their passing is a matter for regret, as are the motor bikes and other machinery that have replaced horses as general farm transport. He has a genuine love of horses and is one of the few farmers still fitting shoes. He would like to give the job away but says it's difficult to say no to a kid riding up to the gate asking, 'Can you please put some new shoes on my pony?' His most touching poem, 'Quincy', is about a young boy who rides his little pony out to rescue his father who is injured and trapped by a bushfire.

For many years a photograph of Ross and his horse Lonely hung on a wall of Naseby's Ancient Briton, one of the town's two hotels. Lonely had once been a savagely wild stallion belonging to Ross's brother who decided the animal would have to be shot. Ross reluctantly agreed but the shooting was postponed when it started to rain; his brother didn't want to get his gun wet. Ross called on his brother during the same afternoon and, finding the young horse still alive, thought it looked rather sad and lonely.

'I was nursing my wife. I was feeling down in the dumps. On the spur of the moment I took the horse home and spent the next two months breaking him in. I often rode Lonely down the hill to town. He was sometimes seen waiting with his reins tied up outside the Ancient Briton.' But, having lived a respectable lifespan, Lonely has gone. 'He was always a bit of an outlaw in his own way. But I really loved old Lonely. And I believe he loved me.'

Naseby, the home of 'Blue Jeans', is a small town — population about 100 — at the end of a road a few kilometres from Ranfurly. It boasts the smallest local body in the South Island, and the highest in New Zealand. The town was named after Naseby in England where a decisive battle was fought between Cromwell and King Charles I in June 1645. Otago's

Naseby was founded when the Parker brothers allegedly discovered gold in the nearby Hogburn in 1863 and the town quickly grew until the population reached 5000:

> *It was calico and canvas in the days of pick*
> *and pan*
> *Where the cry of Gold was magic to the hardy*
> *mining man.*
> *It was huts of mud and tussock, it was streets*
> *of ruts and slush,*
> *And the nights were wild and woolly in the*
> *heyday of the rush.*

More than a century later Naseby can best be described as a scruffy little town, yet it has a captivating atmosphere. Go there for a day, and you can still be there a week later. The town exists for its forestry, local farmers, publicans and a few others. Old buildings have been made from sun-dried bricks, and along walking tracks through the nearby Hogburn Gully, you discover intriguing honey-coloured cliffs, sculptured all those

Watchmaker's Shop in Naseby.

years ago by the gold miners' water-sluicing guns. The Ancient Briton serves as the headquarters for the Otago Central Curling Club, to which Ross McMillan belongs. The curling trophies are also kept in the tavern; the most sought after prize is the Callander Trophy which has been competed for since 1887. At times, Ross says, the curling club has threatened to take over the Ancient Briton, and the publican has been heard to ask whether in fact the pub really belongs to the curlers, and he just pays the rates!

Curling, to many Central Otago people, is more important than rugby. The old Scottish game is like a game of bowls on ice. The rules are even similar, the main difference being that, in bowls, the Jack can be moved, whereas in curling, the 'Pot Lid' (a circle in the ice) cannot. Curling has been played in Naseby since the first club was formed about 127 years ago. The district has four clubs and competition is often fierce. Curling stones, known as 'granites', weigh 16 to 19 kilos each, and a pair is likely to cost over $1000.

Dress is important. Players wear jerseys featuring their club's colours — Ross McMillan and his friends wear royal blue — and hats with pom-poms. And during matches, players are likely to partake of a whisky or two on a variety of excuses. Every July, when the ice is frozen hard, the bonspiel matches — the New Zealand Championships — are played over two days at the nearby town of Oturehua.

The once somewhat male-orientated sport has inspired many lines from 'Blue Jeans'. One of his ballads tells of the liberated curlers who:

> . . . went on strike from the sink and the tub
> And formed themselves into a girls' curling club,
> With an old bloke to coach them and call them 'my girls'
> And teach them the shots that he knows when he curles.
> It made the men laugh as they drank in the bars
> — They'll freeze on the ice now they've burnt up their bras.
> We'll send them back home to the kitchen and sink
> And the kids — were their words as they tossed down a drink.

But one cold night when the girls challenged the men to a game, the men were the losers. Ross McMillan may have been watching the game with mixed emotions: he was the girls' team coach!

'Blue Jeans' also writes about the anguish that a dedicated curler can experience during a seemingly endless Central Otago summer.

> When the summer sun is burning and the days
> are filled with heat,
> Will you know a sudden yearning for black ice
> beneath your feet.
> Will you hear the old stones roaring as your
> lonely job you keep,
> And the shouting of the curlers and the
> swishing of the sweep.

The St Bathans Blue Lake remains as a silent memorial to the gold miners who transformed the landscape.

In my own travels through Central Otago I have enjoyed getting off the main drag in search of unsung heroes. Some small towns still hang on by a thread as illustrious reminders of the 1860s gold rushes. Comparatively huge populations from diminishing goldfields in Victoria, Australia, passed through New Zealand, digging and sluicing for their fortunes, or otherwise, and eventually clearing out for the new promising diggings in California. In their wake remains an appealing legacy of sleepy ghost towns.

A favourite detour and 'Blue Jeans' haunt is a loop road to St Bathans, off Highway 85 between Ranfurly and Alexandra. St Bathans is indeed small, having a population of about 24. Lying in a hollow between the Dunstan and Hawkdun Ranges, it is famous for its attractive Blue Lake dug by the gold miners, and for its historic street featuring the Vulcan Hotel, town hall and post office. Of the three buildings, the Vulcan Hotel is the most auspicious.

Built around 1869 and at one time just one of 13 St Bathans hotels, the Vulcan, with its collections of old relics, is a real gem of the South Island ghost towns. On a good day, many of the St Bathans inhabitants will be seen sitting outside, yarning and enjoying the Otago-brewed beer. And over the years the pub has hit the national news thanks to the friendly ghost supposedly residing in Room 1. A film crew once claimed to have encountered the ghost. They got such a fright they took off without finishing their filming and the story on national television was certainly a boost for the town.

Predictably, the ghost story has been picked up by 'Blue Jeans'. Many St Bathans ghost stories have been told in the pubs around Central Otago and Ross recalls with amusement a time when a Naseby woman spent a night in the Vulcan. 'She said she was scared out of her wits when she awoke in the night and discovered she was being held down. I suggested it was probably her husband. She replied with some indignation, "I know it wasn't him!"'

Ross has given some thought to the identity of the ghost, and he talks about two particular graves in one of the town's two cemeteries. The stones have only the first names of the people buried there. Many folk say it was an Australian gold miner, but Ross McMillan believes it was a saloon girl, 'who never knew true love'. And he always likes to tell the story about a colleague who braved a night in Room 1. 'He was convinced the ghost is a woman. He said he wasn't able to sleep, or get his "tent pole" down all night.' When I asked Ross if he would like to spend a night in Room 1 he replied with a definite no. Then, laughing, he continued, 'Well, not by myself anyway!'

> But folk come from all over
> To bedroom number one
> They speak of saucy doings
> Half in fancy — half in fun.
> Some talk of icy fingers
> And many even boast,
> How in that old-time bedroom
> They've met the Vulcan Ghost.

One summer's evening in Naseby, when I was enjoying a drink in the Ancient Briton with Ross McMillan and other locals, the subject of Naseby's cemetery came into the conversation. One drinker commented

Old timers yarn outside St Bathans' Vulcan Hotel, famous for its Room 1 ghost.

that it was ideally situated on a hill. Another agreed, remarking that 'no one up there's complaining'.

Ross quietly joined the conversation. When he died, he said, he would like it to be in autumn, the most splendid time in Otago. But hopefully that autumn is still some time in the future. He's happy with his lot, and he is still writing his Blue Jeans lines. But, given the choice, he might tell you:

> *I would like to return to the valleys,*
> *Where the frost lay as white as the snow.*
> *To the cattle round up and the rallies,*
> *And the musters we knew long ago.*
> *To the old days, the dash and the dangers,*
> *And the stock camps that stood by the track,*
> *But I know only faces of strangers,*
> *Would meet me if I ventured back.*

The Hang and Glide Birds above Queenstown in Central Otago.

The Hang and Glide Birds

Today was fine and sunny as I went around the sheep.
When I saw movement in the hills — the Kakanuis steep —
I focused the binoculars — then I was stumped for words,
Like from some prehistoric age I saw two giant birds.

Now there are some about no doubt will think this yarn untrue.
And others will be sure to state that I'd been on home brew.
But I saw them in silhouette against the mountain side,
Caught by a balmy updraught they seemed to hang and glide.

They didn't flash across the sky like sparrowhawks in flight.
Not like the oyster catcher or the duck or magpie might.
The sky lark likes to circle, the pigeon likes to race.
But over the Endowment these big birds hung in space.

Far bigger than the heron or the goose and swan their span —
(The body underneath the wings somehow resembled man)
One had a hairy face — the male bird I suppose
Their beaks were red and shiny not unlike the human nose.

I thought of all the musterers to scale the mountain crest,
and wondered why some mountaineer had never found their nest.
The Maori killed the moa off — I guess he didn't know,
About the hang and glide birds that live up in the snow.

So when at last the lambing's done, and I've got some spare time.
All through those rough and lonely hills I mean to probe and climb.
Round cliffs and crags and bluffs of rock — and I'll not spare my legs —
I want to be the first to find some hang and glide bird eggs.

Blue Jeans (Inspired by the first hang gliders seen above Central Otago's mountains.)

Ah Lum Store, a handsome reconstruction in Arrowtown's Chinese village.

LIVING ON THE FRINGE

Ah Lum, a tall Chinese storekeeper with a regal countenance, could be seen each Saturday parading through Arrowtown. He was attired in a long white garment lavishly embroidered at the hem. His arms were folded high across his chest, and a splendid pig-tail hung down from beneath his green tasselled cap.

Such memories have been preserved in Arrowtown's reconstructed Chinese settlement, one of the Otago Goldfields Heritage sites. The collection of reconstructed Chinese dwellings close to Arrowtown's main street is a poignant reminder of the race discrimination experienced last century on the goldfields. Often despised, and forced to exist on the fringe of European settlement, the Chinese nevertheless contributed much to early New Zealand life and culture. Many of today's 25,000 New Zealand Chinese are descended from these early goldfields immigrants. Arrowtown's small St John's Presbyterian church, opened in 1873, is but one legacy of Chinese immigration. It was built with Chinese labour and, on occasions, Chinese comprised half the congregation.

A walk through the reconstructed settlement is an idyllic experience when autumn splashes gold through the trees bordering the nearby

Arrow River. Even so, one feels that the Chinese were banished to one of the cooler sun-deprived sites in the Queenstown vicinity. This can be confirmed in winter when the quaint huts, almost like slightly enlarged dolls' houses among the willows, poplars and hawthorns, sit on snow.

They were reconstructed following an archaeological excavation of the site started in 1983 by the then Lands and Survey Department. Much of the early excavation was done by Neville Ritchie, the Ministry of Works archaeologist involved with the Clyde Dam hydro development. In fact, the MOW funded the initial Arrowtown work as a recompense for a Chinese settlement that has since been drowned in Cromwell's Lake Dunstan.

Nick Clark, a Department of Conservation officer in Queenstown, was involved in the dig and research work for the reconstruction. 'We have a Chinese village we can claim to be authentic,' he said. 'No work was done without good photographs of the original buildings. We had photographs that gave us a very good idea of details such as the thatch work used for roofing.'

Ah Gum's cottage.

Restored toilet, Arrowtown.

Excavation work around some buildings revealed walls up to a metre high. Other sites, such as Ah Lum's general store, were more substantial structures: only about a third of the store needed to be rebuilt. The store, with lofts either side of the entrance, was modelled on similar structures found in China's Canton delta region. It was built in 1883 for a Chinese market gardener, and became a store during the 1890s. 'Ah Lum's store, near the settlement's entrance, is very authentic and is undoubtedly the best of the Otago Chinese sites. There are others, but they are in poor condition, and they are not readily accessible.' Close by, an outdoor long-drop of schist construction, minus its door but otherwise complete, proudly displays its Historic Places Trust preservation plaque.

A variety of building materials — mud brick, cob, canvas and schist slab — is evident, and corrugated iron and thatch serve as roofing. The tiny dwellings are mostly a single room, with no plumbing, yet, in the 1870s they were said to have been 'fit for any European to dwell in'.

In 1866, when the initial Otago gold rush was over, and European miners had left in their thousands for other goldfields, Chinese were

Chinese grave, Naseby.

invited to Otago by the Dunedin Chamber of Commerce. They arrived from Canton, and from the Australian goldfields, prepared to work over abandoned claims. Many later became market gardeners. But the new arrivals were the targets of racist attacks in a New Zealand that was aggressively pro-European and pro-Empire.

Younger Chinese took the opportunity to escape poverty in their home provinces, and later returned with wealth, having earned £100 or more in New Zealand. Such a princely sum is said to have represented 20 years of wages in China. Others were less fortunate. Ah Gum, whose thatch-roofed schist dwelling is arguably the most handsome in the reconstructed village, was found dead at Brackens Gully. The £70 in his pocket was almost all he needed to return home. Many who remained after the turn of the century were the less successful Chinese. As hopes of returning home diminished, they lived out their remaining years in increasingly squalid settlements.

The Reverend Alexander Don, who founded the Presbyterian Chinese church, wondered how they continued to live year after year in those miserable little huts. 'Most of the men are very old and infirm,' he wrote. 'They just live on from day to day, doing nothing, and sleeping much, without God, and without hope.'

Ah Lum's magnificent presence in Arrowtown during the 1920s — he died in 1927 — was the exception. Chinese storekeepers were apparently respected, even by Europeans. More often than not, Ah Lum was followed by coolies carrying ginger jars and baskets of vegetables slung on sticks hung across their shoulders.

The Chinese dominated Arrowtown in the 1880s and the restored settlement, the sole survivor of about 15 others in Otago, reflects a growing interest in New Zealand Chinese immigration. It also serves, in a small way, as a panacea for the discrimination practised against these gentle people all those years ago.

CHAPTER 13

THE LUCKIEST MAN IN THE RAILWAY

The heart of the railway system I once loved has all gone. I'm still here, running my own steam railway.

Russell Glendinning

In a sense I celebrated my millennium by re-acquainting myself with a magnificent example of restored steam machinery. Locomotive Ab 795, heading the famous Kingston Flyer tourist train, was climbing the grade out of Kingston at the southern end of Lake Wakatipu, bound for Fairlight about 14 kilometres away. And I was attached to the T-handle of the fireman's long-bladed coal shovel, aiming coal at an all too small firehole while the footplate rolled relentlessly under my feet. Perhaps old Ab 795, built in Dunedin in 1927, deserved better than me as she steamed confidently and proudly through the first days of a new century. But I was doing my best, and the funnel talk from the Ab was impressive.

'Hang onto that shovel,' shouted veteran railwayman Russell Glendinning who had been with the Flyer since its beginning, 29 years before.

It was a long, long, throw getting the coal to the front of the firebox. The professional railwaymen had made it all look so easy. At last I straightened my aching back and looked at Russell's bemused smile as he shut the firebox door. For my rookie efforts he offered a 4 out of 10, but promised to consider a 7 or 8 if my fire produced sufficient steam to reach Fairlight.

Steve, the young driver hanging onto the throttle and whistle cord, was working towards his fully fledged steam-locomotive driver's ticket. He had a special whistle for his girlfriend who lived on a farm bordering the track. As the train passed she was often seen by Kingston Flyer passengers, riding a white horse or a farm bike. It all seemed romantic until Russell revealed the true story of forbidden love. The girl's father, disapproving of the fledgling relationship, had apparently threatened the young Kingston Flyer driver unless he kept away from his daughter. For a moment I could have believed this was the Wild West — and indeed the Kingston Flyer was the centrepiece of the famous Crunchie Bar train shoot-out filmed in 1973, and believed to be the world's longest-running television advertisement.

But with my back bent low over shovel after shovel of heavy coal, any thoughts of collecting an angry farmer's bullet were secondary to the task of covering 33 square feet (3 square metres) of firebox belonging to this vibrant old steam locomotive. I had no idea so much hand-shovelled coal was needed to make a steam locomotive travel even a short distance. But soon I was getting the hang of it, swinging my body in one movement, spreading the coal evenly and covering the thin parts of the fire, and watching the steam pressure gauge hover just under the line marking 150 pounds. Any more, and the hard-won steam would shoot skywards from the safety valve simmering away behind a polished

Russell Glendinning with his Ab 795. 'I have seen New Zealand's railways in the heyday of steam.'

Driver/fireman Steve firing up Ab 795 for another trip to Fairlight.

brass steam dome. And I kept a firm grip on Russell Glendinning's shovel, hand-shaped by a lifetime of stoking ravenous locomotive fires.

If my role in the Kingston Flyer that January day was insignificant (and for the record we did reach Fairlight with a gratifying reserve of steam), the same could not be said for Russell Glendinning. He is rightly known as 'Mr Kingston Flyer'.

'There's no other preserved steam railway like it in New Zealand,' he says. 'Other steam railways have been created, but this is as original as you could get it. We haven't had to create anything. We still run on rails laid in 1878 and we look at the same mountains. We're maintaining a small portion of an old branch line. The tourist train just fits into what was already here. That's the real passion of the Flyer. And we're a commercial operation with a 60 per cent increase in revenue over the past eight years.'

The Kingston Flyer operation has two Ab class locomotives with the famous Pacific 4-6-2 wheel arrangement. The other, Ab 778, was built at the former Addington Railway Workshops, Christchurch, in 1925. Both locos are presented in a 1920s style with glossy black paint, white-rimmed driving wheels, red-fluted side rods and a wealth of polished brass. Passengers ride in seven veteran carriages built between 1899 and 1923 and finished in the former New Zealand Railways Pullman green livery with gold lining. An old 'birdcage' carriage is especially popular. It all looks superb. 'But the rolling stock is getting a little creaky in joints, like me,' says Russell Glendinning. 'We potter. But we don't have to wear ourselves out racing along the main line.'

Russell, a tall, patient man with a kindly smile, has been working with the same two steam locomotives since 1971. 'You get attached to them after that amount of time. Of course you do. They also frustrate you. They try you to the limit when it comes to repair work. But you don't like things going wrong. When a steam locomotive isn't going right it's like having a sick grandmother. You don't like to see her sick.'

The Kingston Flyer could be associated only with the South Island. The name originated early last century when it was applied to a so-called crack express that began running between Gore on the South Island Main Trunk, and Kingston, in November 1902. Connecting at Kingston with Lake Wakatipu steamers, the train boosted tourism in Queenstown. The Kingston Flyer service was discontinued in 1937 but the track it ran on continued as a branch line, eventually providing the permanent way for New Zealand's only steam-powered commercial tourist train.

The present Kingston Flyer tourist train began in 1971, working on a longer section of track between Kingston and Lumsden. It was the brainchild of the then New Zealand Railways general manager Ivan Thomas, and Minister of Railways Peter Gordon. In 1970 the two men travelled south to hear submissions against the proposed closing of the branch line and on the return flight to Wellington they hit on the idea of the tourist train as a means to make the railway viable. The Kingston Flyer, launched the following year, was a success from day one. Passenger loadings exceeded expectations, the Kingston Flyer picked up tourism awards and its senior driver, Russell Glendinning, was awarded the MBE for his services to tourism and industry.

But despite its undoubted success, the Flyer was suddenly doomed. In 1979 the government of the day claimed, somewhat unfairly, that the train was not paying its way. A disappointed community watched as the Kingston Flyer departed for the last time before leaving to run between Invercargill and Bluff. 'The relocation lasted only two years and was a disaster,' Russell recalls.

In the meantime, Wakatipu locals, mostly farmers, fought to retain the railway facilities — the water tank at Kingston in particular — in the hope that their Flyer might one day return. So when a demolition gang arrived to dismantle the water tank a few days before Christmas 1979,

An immaculate Ab 778 heading the Kingston Flyer in style between Fairlight and Kingston.

they were confronted by an angry picket. Within a short time, however, an agreement was struck. The locals, having picked up a few tips from the unions, declared the tank 'black', and the workers refused to touch it. The story hit the national headlines, and the government relented.

The Kingston Flyer did return, in December 1982, albeit on a shorter length of track and run by a Queenstown consortium, Kingston Flyer Ltd. Then, following the sale of the New Zealand Railways in 1993 to the Tranz Rail consortium, the Flyer once again became part of the national rail system.

'For many years the Flyer slowly lost its credibility with the tourist industry,' says Russell Glendinning. 'Tourist operators will often make bookings two years, or more, ahead. You need to tell people you will still be here. If you can't do that they're not interested. We now have bookings five years ahead. And that has a lot to do with the Tranz Rail commitment to the Flyer.'

Russell claims the Kingston Flyer as New Zealand's premier vintage railway operation. 'Unlike preservation groups that rely on volunteer labour, we have to pay people. Enthusiast groups also get grants from the Lotterie Commission. We can't because we're a commercial railway.'

But as I was attempting to provide sufficient steam for old Ab 795, Russell Glendinning was considering his own role in a new millennium. At the age of 63 he has been thinking about adding other interests to his life. He has a love for the sea — and roses. He is a volunteer ambulance officer, local game warden and harbourmaster.

'I want to pursue other things close to my heart. I've always had a yearning for the history of roses and propagating. You never know what you can do till you do it. Most people have got more than one talent. I'm lucky to have a job I still enjoy doing. All my life has been with the Railways. I still enjoy it.'

His railway career began with scrubbing toilets in Dunedin 48 years ago. 'My grand ideas of becoming an engine driver were dispelled in

The Kingston Flyer headed by Ab 778 climbing out of Kingston, seen in the background beside Lake Wakatipu. (Photograph John Brouwer)

my first 10 minutes. I was given a bucket, a mop and scrubbing brush, and told to clean toilets. I was brought down to earth with a thud.'

But not for long. Russell progressed to become an engine cleaner and, eventually, senior driver at Bluff. In between, he worked on every branch line, and in every depot south of Oamaru. 'I've seen the railway in its heyday of steam and when railways went to places like Ranfurly, Cromwell and Roxburgh. I've done everything I wanted to do on the railway. Otago and Southland hung onto their pioneering branch lines to the end. It's basically only main trunk running now. The heart of the railway system I once loved has all gone now. I'm still here, running my own steam railway. I have no regrets at all. Not one.'

He was one of 26 people in the running for the Kingston Flyer job in 1971 and he applied so he could pursue his love of steam.

'It's the mystery and complexity of the machine. It's huge, black, and alive with things flying around. It still attracts kids today. You see them standing in awe of the thing. It overawes everything else. An aircraft, or ship, is either big or small. It looks nice. But there's no mystery. There's not many people who wouldn't stop and look at a steam train moving away. A kid the other day followed me when I was working around the Ab with an oil can. He said, "I'd like to be you, mister." And this, even in the computer age.

Fairlight at the end of the line.

The Luckiest Man in the Railway

Visiting touring cyclists from the Netherlands and Ab 795 at Fairlight.

'I talk to a lot of school groups and I still get asked the same questions as I did when I started with the Flyer almost 30 years ago. They want to know how fast it goes? How much coal does it use? How hot is the fire, and why does the smoke go up the front, when the fire is in the back?'

And he is hot on his loco staff wearing uniforms, including a white tie, which is an old railway tradition. 'If you wore a clean tie then you had a cleaner engine than the next crew. It was a matter of pride.' The white tie was made from an old sheet and Russell admits it was often retied during the day to show a clean bit above the overalls. 'And you always had a spare clean one in your pocket.'

The Kingston Flyer, on the main route between Queenstown, Te Anau and Milford Sound is focused on tourism, which brings new passengers every day. That is why it is successful: It does not have to rely on the same source of people as it would do if the steam train was based anywhere else.

'And it is so well established in this part of the South Island. You talk about the Kingston Flyer, and people associate it with a place. Kingston is a very small town at one end of Lake Wakatipu. If you put the Flyer into Auckland it wouldn't mean anything. It would just be another steam train.' We both almost choke on our coffee when we contemplate this beautiful train becoming 'The Auckland Flyer'. 'And we take historic connections back to the beginning, to the first passenger links between the South Island Main Trunk and the lakes district.'

A glance through the visitors' book confirms that tourists love the Kingston Flyer. The old steam railway falls outside the hurly-burly of the tourist circuit and its associated high-pressure timetables. For Russell, the train represents a return to normality.

'All of a sudden people get on this dear old steam train, sit down with a cup of coffee, and they go back 50 years. We don't care if we depart five minutes late because we wait for someone to get a camera that's been left on the bus. That's the attraction of it. Most steam train operations are well known for not being in a hurry. To us, the timetable is secondary to what people want. Even if we want to get home at the end of a long 12-hour shift, we'll still stop to talk to someone.'

Russell has a fund of memories of those who have enjoyed the Kingston Flyer. He recalls a man from Alaska who asked if his boy could have a ride on the loco. 'I said, "Of course he can." He said, "That's great. I've been to steam railways around the world and you can't get near the loco, let alone ride on it."

Then there was the 98-year-old tourist who wanted to ride on the footplate. 'Took us five minutes to get him on the loco, and another 10 minutes to get him off at the other end. He said he had been to Milford Sound, but he would never forget the Kingston Flyer.'

One group of well-heeled people had chartered an aircraft to fly to New Zealand. It was an annual event: the previous year they had been to Egypt where they ended up dining with gold cutlery in a palace. 'Here they ate with plastic knives and forks. They were being treated like ordinary people, and taking us just as we were because we couldn't change. And all this in a beautiful lakeside setting. We had trouble getting them off the train at the end of their trip. They just didn't want to go.

'This is the Kingston Flyer. We can't provide coffee and service like the Ritz. Even our 100-year-old dunnies are an attraction, and our gas lights. But the gas lights aren't used. They might blow up. Carriage lighting is provided from a generator on the locomotive.'

Tourism can be fickle. If a booking is turned down you never get another from that company: It is a matter of always meeting expectations. In this respect the Kingston Flyer is fortunate in being part of a system that has an international name for its Tranz Scenic rail journeys. 'The Flyer is definitely something positive. Some people may perceive Tranz Rail as just another heartless corporation. But the Kingston Flyer shows there's still a weak spot,' he laughs.

But at the heart of the Kingston Flyer are two Ab class steam locomotives working on an isolated section of railway, and you cannot just drive them to a repair depot. Everything has to be done in a workshop at Kingston that does not have electricity. Russell has to rely on the old skills he learned during his apprenticeship days. 'They're still usable here, and they can be passed on to younger people.'

During the winter of 1999 he stripped an Ab down. The locomotive was lifted up and the wheels, axle boxes, and running gear were taken away for a complete undergear overhaul. Some of the subsequent work was done by Tranz Rail's Hutt workshops, and some by local engineering. 'Older ideas often have to be adapted to get a big job done. It's time consuming. And crane hire is expensive. It will cost about $1000 to get a crane up from Invercargill, and that's before any work is started.'

The Ab class, he says, was one of the better locomotives on the New Zealand Railways: it was so much down the middle of the road, it would go anywhere and do anything, it was economical and it was fast enough.

When he started with the Kingston Flyer as senior driver at Lumsden, he was responsible only for running the train to Kingston and back.

After 29 years, Russell Glendinning is still trundling on with the Flyer. But he says it is time to add other interests to his life.

These days, as area manager, he is in charge of the entire railway operation, including administration, track maintenance and even occasionally washing the buffet dishes. 'We have five full-time staff and we all muck in.

'But I never thought I'd ever be responsible for running a railway. Sometimes I have to pinch myself to believe it's true. If I want to run the Kingston Flyer at 1 o'clock, or 5 o'clock, that's what I do. It's a luxury. I have my own train. It's a nice feeling, sometimes, knowing I can keep it running. That's part of the success of the Flyer.

'And I know that if I tried to walk away from it, in five minutes I'd be back. I'm the luckiest man in the railway.'

North

CHAPTER 14

WINNING WAYS WITH WINE

*Farming's social life had died. Wine has
taken me off on a totally new tangent . . .*
John McCaskey

John McCaskey can afford to look a little smug. Sometime during the 1960s the Waipara farmer believed the arid land in his part of the South Island would grow wine grapes. The countryside was prone to suffer a succession of droughts — in one year, the rainfall was a mere 280 millimetres — but in those days, he says, the bank managers would have laughed him out of town had he talked about a vineyard. Back then, New Zealand had a handful of winemakers — less than 100 for the entire country — and no one had much faith in Waipara.

As it was, his first venture into grape growing, in 1965, was literally a washout. He acquired heaps of old variety grape cuttings from a neighbour who had them decorating a glasshouse. 'I planted them up by Weka Creek in nice silty ground, put netting around and got them struck. Next thing a good flood went walloping through. That was the end of that. They're probably growing in the Chathams somewhere.'

Times have changed. Waipara is now a small but burgeoning wine-producing region and John McCaskey alone has won about 35 medals in a little over a decade for his Glenmark Wines. In 1986, in a hayshed, he made Waipara's first wine from his own vineyard, and from that vintage he won a medal for his now famous Waipara Red. He is often, with justification, called the father of the Waipara wine industry, but he has also been christened the Barry Crump of New Zealand wine. His blunt down-to-earth manner, allied with a lean frame and weather-beaten farmer's face, does not fit the modern-day winemakers' social set. As he says with a laugh, 'someone had to break the mould.'

And the Barry Crump image doesn't worry him at all. 'If somebody puts you in line with someone who's pretty much an icon for many

New Zealanders, why should you object? Of course some people saw another side of Crump and didn't like him for his marriage falling apart and so on, but I don't suppose my history is a hell of a lot different.'

He suspects the image was derived from an interview for a wine magazine and another for a book about boutique wineries. The accompanying photograph in the book was reproduced quite dark, making the most of John's weather-beaten face. And he suspects he made a few of his somewhat blunt remarks during the interviews.

He has struggled through years when droughts and successive government policies 'ripped the guts' out of the rural community. 'For the first time in my life, in a few weeks, I don't owe anyone anything,'

John McCaskey, pioneer winemaker, is still looking for new varieties for Waipara soils.

he says. 'I'm my own man. It's been a long, long, haul.' And to prove the worth of the struggle, from an unlabeled bottle, he pours two glasses of Proprietor's 1999 Reserve Riesling.

Back in 1960 John McCaskey set out on his Big OE. He spent some time in Australia working for Melbourne company Conner-Shea, involved in agricultural machinery. Then, during a second trip to Australia in 1965, he piloted a Cessna up through the centre of Australia, flying his old boss. 'We went up as far as Darwin, but on the way we stopped in at Mildura where the guys from the CSIRO [Commonwealth Scientific and Industrial Research Organisation] gave me a conducted tour of the vineyards, and we talked about the research they were doing.'

He saw similarities between the climate on the border of Victoria and New South Wales, and his home at Waipara. 'Two things survive in drought conditions, and pop up when the going gets good. One is livestock. And grapes struck me as being the other. Down the Rhine in Germany you see pictures of grapes hanging onto rock on the side the river. In Australia, they were growing in arid conditions which meant that soil appeared to be only part of the equation. Heat units, the length of season and a supply of water were other essentials.'

And he knew about the Waipara bubble, the micro-climate caused by heat accumulating in the Weka Pass during the day and drifting out over the flat, with its dry stony soils, at night. In 1961 he had introduced bulk contract harvesting to New Zealand and he harvested properties from Amberley north to the Greta Valley. 'Driving around in a harvester at night you get to know where warm spots are. Once any dampness comes in you have to stop. I often harvested in Waipara all night. Less than 10 kilometres either way, and I couldn't do it.' One spring night he was out late spraying copper for frost protection. 'As I drove around the vineyard the air movement was just enough to dampen me with spray drift. It wasn't that cold. But Amberley had a stinking frost that night.'

Tomatoes grown from seedlings in an open field were the forerunner to grape growing. 'Bob Crowder, the horticulture guru at Lincoln, was looking for somewhere to grow tomatoes. He was convinced that Waipara, being dry and arid, was as near to a Californian climate as you would find anywhere in New Zealand. The only ingredient lacking always was water. It was hopeless to grow tomatoes without it. So early in 1972 I put in a little storage dam, shot up to the top of the farm, put a pump into the creek, got a water right, and excavated a dam down by the homestead. It was then just a matter of jumping on the tractor with a plough behind, and putting a furrow down the farm. I just let the water run down and waited for the dam to fill.'

His father had tried to irrigate the Weka plain during the mid-1930s, but it was not until the mid-1980s that the Glenmark irrigation scheme was eventually established.

The first tomatoes were harvested in 1973. Then in 1976 they took 33 tonnes off 0.8 hectare where the vineyard is now established. Tomatoes have been grown in Waipara ever since. 'Trouble was there were no tomato harvesters, apart from people on bended knees picking the darn things,' John says ruefully. 'But we had determined that Waipara could be frost-free from Labour Weekend, when we planted them, through to Easter when we got them all harvested. And there had to be sufficient sunshine to ripen them.

'The tomato experiment proved the Californian climate theory because that's where they're grown in thousands of acres. It also suggested that the season was long enough for grape growing. And we could probably be relatively frost-free through the danger period for grapes, from bud-burst in mid-October till late April.'

Winemaking in Waipara might have started earlier, but agricultural colleges and farmers were interested only in sheep: wool and fat lambs were making them enough money. 'It was only when the economic situation changed and the wine fanatics — people like David Jackson, Danny Schuster and one or two others — started up that it began to be taken seriously. By then Montana and winemaking in Marlborough were rolling.'

In hindsight, he says, it would have been wonderful to have been growing wine grapes during the 1960s. 'Even if it would have been all the wrong sort of grapes, at least we would have been making bag-in-the-box wine. We would have had our feet on ground, and having a go at it.'

When he did start his vineyard, boutique wineries were already doing something different, and going for the top of the market. Even so, people stared in wonder. 'McCaskey's growing grapes,' they said shaking their heads in wonder. 'What's he going to do with them?'

'We were growing Riesling, Cabernet Sauvignon and some others in those days. But I said nothing to the bank. I would have been asked why I was doing such a crazy thing, and what was I doing spending money I didn't have anyway?'

Others, led by the politician Derek Quigley, had established a syndicate to grow grapes in Waipara and were getting quite a bit of publicity for their efforts. 'They were supplying wine grapes to one of the big wine producers in Blenheim. The obvious thing was for me to do the same. But the quantities I was producing weren't worth transporting that far, and I doubt anybody would have been interested in buying them anyway.'

But John McCaskey has never been one for doing the obvious thing. When visiting the United States a friend who had taken an interest in the McCaskey vineyard let slip that there was this guy way down in New Zealand growing grapes and he wanted to start a winery.

'Next thing I get a phone call from this stranger who said he was Steve Harber. He said "I hear you want a winemaker down there?" He then went on, "Well, I'm not actually a qualified winemaker but I've been a cellar rat for 15 years. 'I'll make the wine for you if you want to go along with it." Steve had no professional qualification, other than lots of experience. We harvested the grapes — the Riesling and the Waipara White — and we tramped the red with our feet in some dairy vats. Lo and behold, the week before we opened the winery we heard our Waipara Red had won a bronze metal in the Air New Zealand wine awards.'

Glenmark Waipara Red sells for about $15 a bottle, the same as it did

Glenmark Wines, winning medals over a selection of red and white grape varieties.

in 1986. The basic blending of Cabernet Sauvignon and Pinot is similar, but John McCaskey has been experimenting with 'tippling in' small quantities of Merlot and Malbec. Merlot provides the beautiful soft flavour. Malbec gives the colour. As I understand it, it's a Bordeaux-style wine.

He believes that, despite the hype, South Island vineyards are not getting the big success with Cabernet Sauvignon. 'Sure, there have been some good seasons, and it's great. But out in my vineyard Cabernet Franc is setting every year. They're nice clean grapes. The Merlot sets a light crop and ripens up beautifully, as does the Malbec. They're light crops but you only need small quantities to put with the other. I see them as future blending grapes, with Cabernet Franc or Cabernet Sauvignon giving the bulk.'

Building the Glenmark winery was an interesting exercise. Again, John simply did not have any money at a time when having stainless steel tanks made for a winery was costing about a dollar a litre. A reasonably-sized wine tank was about 9000 litres, and Glenmark needed storage for an annual production of 20,000 litres. 'Two large beer tankers were at Timaru, having finished their life on the road,' he recalls. 'So I borrowed a truck's tractor unit and made two trips to Timaru to drag them home.' The beer tankers were pushed into a haybarn where they became the wine tanks for the first couple of years.

'But we thought upright tanks would have us looking a little more sophisticated. We heard the United Services Hotel was finishing in Cathedral Square. We rushed down there with a chainsaw one Saturday morning and cut a hole in the floor. We hauled the beer tanks out, put them on a trailer and off we went. We converted each of them into wine tanks, complete with a porthole in the side. Even those somewhat compromised wine tanks were expensive in those days.'

For John McCaskey, growing wine grapes was initially just another farmer's crop, and the work involved in establishing a vineyard was not unlike traditional farm fencing. These days he sees a very different scene. 'People are coming in with a big income outside of farming. They buy a block of land and have the capital to whack in a really nice tidy operation. And they're prepared to wait a few years before getting an income off it. I was doing it out of what I could find from the almost non-existent farming income.'

Glenmark Winery opened four years ahead of the second winery in

Dressed for the occasion, John McCaskey at opening day for the Weka Pass Railway in September 1999. He was one of the instigators of the railway's reopening.

the area, Waipara Springs. Glenmark wines continued to win awards for John McCaskey — not for a particular variety, but across a range of red and white wines. 'The awards meant the Waipara region had credibility. They demonstrated we could produce top Chardonnay, Riesling, and Gewürztraminer, along with Cabernet Sauvignon and Pinot Noir.'

With credibility came the bigger investors. By the year 2000 Waipara was boasting about 11 wine producers, all producing some world-class wines. 'Canterbury House fills the skyline as you approach Waipara from the south. It's making a positive statement. It is there to say how much faith someone has in the Waipara wine industry.

'A good spin-off from the newer wine producers is the diversity of professions and the jobs that have been attracted to Waipara. But it's a far cry from the days when we had dreams just to do something different.'

In a sense John McCaskey is a junior version of the legendary winemaker, Murray Tyrrell, of Australia's Hunter Valley. In 1967 Tyrrell returned from a trip to France, keen to grow Chardonnay. In those days Australia offered only two small vineyards growing the variety; one belonged to Penfolds who were reluctant to sell. According to Murray Tyrrell's own account of events, with help from a willing Penfolds employee, he helped himself to 1100 cuttings one moonlit night. From those cuttings Tyrrell's Winery produced Australia's first successful oak-aged Chardonnay, and began to collect a heap of gold medals from Australian wine shows.

John McCaskey's attempt to do something a little questionable didn't come off. If it had, he admits it might have earned him a few black marks but, even so, he still harbours some regrets.

'In 1965, coming back from Australia, I fully intended to bring some cuttings from Mildura. We were looking at Chardonnay grapes when the CSIRO scientist said, "You're a bit cooler in New Zealand. I think these will grow well." He gave me some cuttings which I took great care of. But when I was half-way back across the Tasman I realised I had walked out and left them behind in the fridge.'

I have met up with John McCaskey on many occasions, starting in the early 1980s when he was gunning for the restoration of the Weka Pass Railway where trains, on their way from Waipara to Waikari, now trundle past his Glenmark vineyard. Later I was involved in a newspaper piece when he won a gold medal for a 1991 Chardonnay he produced with winemaker Kym Rayner.

But when I caught up with him again in the spring of 2000 he was the happiest I had seen him in years. He still had his archetypal 'Barry Crump' edge. And he was even leaner, and his face more lined. But somehow, he looked confident. It would be another two weeks before he found out if the Waipara Red had secured a medal in the Air New Zealand Awards.

These days John McCaskey is his own winemaker. He is still keen to experiment, and to learn from past experiences. He talks about his early white wines when most varieties were 'tipped into the one bucket' to become his Waipara White. Later he separated the varieties to produce top Rieslings, Gewürztraminers and Chardonnays. Waipara White, these days, is predominately Müller Thurgau.

The German grape Reichensteiner was a 'bit of a disaster' as he recalls only too well. 'Just as the grapes were ripening up (a couple of weeks ahead of the others), the birds said, "Hello, it's feed time" and stripped the vines. That variety got the chainsaw!'

Much more successful has been a small planting of Pinot Gris. Over 18 years it has never failed to give a crop. 'It suits the hot and dry Waipara climate and it is almost disease-free. The skin is fairly hard like a Riesling. And the birds don't like it. And at the end of the day, you have a magic wine. Pinot Gris is a wine I would like to go down the track with.' He

The Weka Pass Railway's A 428 arriving at Waikari on 11 September 1999.

would also like to have a go at growing Shiraz, the famous big red that does so well in Australia. He thinks Waipara could produce the grape on light stony ground.

New Zealand has made an international name for white wines, particularly Sauvignon Blanc and Chardonnay. But John McCaskey hears international commentators saying something about New Zealand reds.

'Back in 1986 everybody was used to big gutsy Australian Cabernets that blew the top off your head, and you really wanted to chain them up for a couple of years before you used them — a bit like blue-vein cheese. You let it out of its cage when it's ready. Now, people are getting used to New Zealand reds that are much more subtle. They don't have to whack you in the back of the throat with flavours. Pinot Noir, a delicate red, has probably been the leader in this respect.'

Whatever image the industry may wish to give him, John McCaskey has undoubtedly joined the ranks of the so-called wine fanatics. The wine medals he has won have seen to that. He believes the key to the continuing success of New Zealand viticulture is held by the small boutique wineries.

'New Zealand's winemakers have tripled since I started. We now have about 350 winemakers. Out of those, about 300 are small wineries, or small businesses, looking for the top-shelf price. If we sell our wine at $10 a bottle we're never going to make it. We just haven't got the economy of scale — even to supply bottles or have the labels turned out. Economies of scale pass us by.

'We now have "the flying winemaker" and a globalisation of styles. These are winemakers who can make a vintage in France, fly to Chile to make another, then on to other regions including Australia and New Zealand. In one sense it's wonderful. But they're stamping their style on that country, or that particular valley. It may result in, say, Bulgarian Chardonnays tasting the same as Australian Chardonnays, or New Zealand's, albeit with subtle differences.

'For this reason the little people need to survive. They're the innovators. They want to stamp their individuality. In the big bulk tanks everything ends up much the same. But in little barrels, at a little winery at the back of places like Waipara, the wine is distinctly different. Small wine producers will always be experimenting.'

The Pinot Noir groups we have in New Zealand are a classic example. If someone moved in with 200 hectares of Pinot Noir, the market might soon be swamped and the variety would lose its mystique. 'Waipara, Central Otago and Martinborough are the Pinot Noir enthusiasts. They want to unlock its secrets; they want to make it in a particular way that large producers have probably got no show of emulating.'

'I'll never be sorry I got into wine growing. It's exciting and it's added another dimension to life. We've lost the rural community spirit I grew up with. The Saturday night dances disappeared when the hotel cult took over with later closing, and people didn't have to invent their own fun.

'Farming's social life has died. Wine has taken me off on a totally new tangent, going to wine tastings and being a salesman of the product I produce. I have always said to myself, whatever I do I want total control from what I grow to the finished product. Completely go to whoa.

'When we were growing a paddock of wheat, or raising lambs, it always struck me that farmers got shafted. We were just price takers, and we saw flour millers and butchers make a rake off which seemed to be out of proportion to the work we did.'

In the meantime John McCaskey wants his Glenmark Wines to retain its modest 20,000 litres a year production. Over the years he has sold off land to other winegrowers and small block holdings. He has also purchased additional blocks. At present he is planning a new vineyard and wine garden restaurant at the end of the road. He will name the new venture House o' Hill, representing a link with his family history. House o' Hill is the name of a small pub in Bargrennan, Dumfries, Scotland where his maternal great, great, grandfather McLaren was the innkeeper. McLaren's family emigrated to Leithfield, and later farmed at Cheviot. 'We then had three generations who skipped being involved with the booze, but my role in the hospitality industry is somewhat more refined,' John laughs.

So up at the end of the road a once-cherished family tradition will be restored. There may be time to think about a nine-hole golf course. 'That will be my last burst, I guess. When we started planting wine grapes in '81 everyone expected the whole lot to soon fall over.'

CHAPTER 15

HOME IS WHERE THE HEART IS

You can't change who you are, or the way you were brought up. But I love this place. I'll never leave here. This is it.

Mary Nepia

Mary Nepia is in love with her Waikari Valley. 'Living here beats town living,' she says while taking a break from her customers at The Yorkshire Teapot. 'We get a lot of people from England stopping off here. Once they see the sign from the top of the hill as they come down from the Weka Pass, they're onto their brakes wanting to find out about this little tearoom with "Yorkshire" in its name. Sometimes it can be very noisy with a crowd of people, all from the north of England.'

Mary, a diminutive busy woman with a wonderful laugh, grew up among the woollen mills of Yorkshire's old West Riding. Despite her years in New Zealand, 25 of them in Waikari, she still speaks with a distinctive Yorkshire lilt. As her surname suggests, she married a New Zealander, 'but the marriage didn't last,' she says ruefully. What has lasted is her love for her valley.

Waikari is one of the smaller hamlets in North Canterbury. 'It's a nice life here. The pace isn't fraught like it is in those big city malls. And where else can you get views like we have from every window. If it was California you'd be paying millions of dollars for the views we have!' She sees similarities between the Yorkshire Dales and her North Canterbury valley. 'Over there we looked out onto the Pennines. Here, it's the wonderful Puketeraki Range.'

Her spotless tearoom is a delight to visit, and I make a point of stopping for a cup of tea or coffee whenever I travel to Hanmer Springs, or take the Lewis Pass route to the West Coast or Nelson. Mary talks with pride about her 60-year-old till which the kids, especially, love. It still works if the electricity fails. On one wall is a painting showing a

Mary Nepia, in love with her Waikari Valley.

famous locomotive, a Single Fairlie R 28, being shifted along a Reefton Street to its final resting place. It is one of two paintings by a Yorkshireman, Peter Findlay, put in the shop several years ago to sell. Mary let one go, but not the other. 'I've always loved that picture. People are always telling me "That's me on the train." Or, "That's my grandfather."' Another delight is a drawing a customer gave her showing a zebra unwinding its stripes. 'It reminds me of Aucklanders and all their stress.'

She talks about Kiwis losing their way. She admires John McCaskey, the rough and ready Waipara winemaker. 'He's a treasure to talk to. We've gone through all the bad times here. He was the first to start a vineyard. His father was the first to make a water race for irrigation. Nobody wanted to know about it in those days, did they? Now it's all the people with the big money who are coming in.'

When I ask Mary if times have been difficult for her my question is answered with an unexpected outburst. 'Of course! Of course! Nineteen eighty-two was shocking. And 1984 was shocking. Don't you remember the big interest rates? All the farmers were closing their chequebooks, and the stock firms were closing? Then we had 1987, and then we had 1990, and then 1992. They were all bad years for the rural community.

'But I've hung on. You've got to, don't you? People want to come in and make a fortune in two years. They're crazy. I talk about selling, but people ask, "Would we get our money back in two years?" Makes you laugh, doesn't it?'

A recent boon has been the reopening of the Weka Pass Railway from Waipara to Waikari. 'People get off the train here. The men can pop into the pub across the road while the women come in here for a cuppa.' And business has picked up with the burgeoning number of travellers, many of them tourists, on the road. Waikari might be a tiny town but Mary says some days 'it's like a grand prix out there'.

Even on a busy Saturday she is happy to talk about her valley and the people who have made her life memorable. There was an 'old

A drawing depicting stress is a laughing point at The Yorkshire Teapot.

The painting of locomotive R 28 at Reefton that Mary Nepia does not want to sell.

chappie' from Hanmer Springs who told her about the day Monty stopped in the valley. Monty was, of course, the 1st Viscount Montgomery of Alamein, the famous English field marshal who drove Rommel's forces back to Tunis in 1942.

'It was 1947, I think he said, or '48? Monty must have been visiting the diggers he'd fought with in the North African desert during the Second World War. He was on his way to Hanmer Springs and when he saw this valley from the top of the hill he asked if he could stop. He then came down to the town and talked to the men lined up outside the Star and Garter to see him.

'Monty apologised for the delay, the old chappie from Hanmer said. But I didn't think Monty had it in him to stop and admire a lovely valley. When we were children we saw him once or twice waving from the back of a train as we toured England. He seemed such a severe man. And just imagine. In 1947 there wouldn't have been much here, would there? There's very little here now. It was the view he stopped for — like I still do.'

She talks about her tearoom being called 'The' Yorkshire Teapot. 'It's not just "Yorkshire Teapot". That would not be grammatically correct.

And it doesn't sound right. But people don't think about that. There's all sorts of errors in the newspaper that there never used to be. People don't worry so much about pronunciation either. So what does that tell you?'

Whenever Mary says she is going to retire, people keep telling her, 'It won't be the same without you.' Or, 'What are we going to do when you go?' She just says, 'Well, I'm still around, aren't I?'

After arriving in New Zealand she spent three years living in a Maori pa. 'I was a woman from Yorkshire. Can you imagine that? It wasn't a matter of liking it. I had to! And I was pregnant at the time. It was a great education, let's put it that way. But I loved the people.' She had left her family behind in England, but 'you either get on with your life or go under. There's no in-between.'

Later she worked in hospitals: she was in charge of the nurses' homes at Seaview and Westland. She recalls her first visit to Waikari and stopping at a small tearoom with dusty shelves and a dusty counter.

The Yorkshire Teapot, a neat tearoom at Waikari in North Canterbury.

Another decade went by, during which the shelves and the counter presumably gathered even more dust. Then she bought the tearooms so she could retire in Waikari and enjoy the view. 'I thought it will never make any money. But retiring. Now, that's a joke.'

She says she will always be a Yorkshire woman. 'You can't change who you are, or the way you were brought up. But I love this place. I'll never leave here. This is it. But I've been able to do as I like in New Zealand without the family saying all the time, "Oh I wouldn't do this, or I wouldn't do that."'

Finally Mary says she must go and do the ice creams. Everything needs filling up for the next wave of people stopping; there could even be an unexpected busload. 'So I can't talk to you any more,' she says with mock defiance.

'But isn't life so interesting,' she says as I leave. 'These last 25 years in my valley have been my best years. I've never had so many laughs.'

CHAPTER 16

TALL TALES AND FINE FISH

People have become so negative. What we need is a damn good laugh.

Daryl Crimp

As Daryl Crimp will tell you, 'All fisherman are born liars, and everyone is a fisherman at heart.' Better known as Crimpy, the Nelson cartoonist, radio host and one-time mad chef will also have you believe that landing one's first trout on an artificial fly is not too dissimilar to one's first sexual encounter. 'Both are pursued with youthful exuberance despite any technique lacking in finesse.'

He once bought a Nelson restaurant, the Brown House, and just before it opened realised he couldn't afford a chef. 'I had just three days to learn. It was difficult.' He partially mastered six recipes before opening day. When things went wrong, as they frequently did, he would appear in the dining room with his chef's hat and stage a Faulty Towers-style act. He was soon dubbed the 'Mad Chef' and the restaurant became an unlikely success.

His cartooning had an equally unlikely beginning. Year after year his Tapawera High School reports said, 'Could do better.' He was no good at maths, but one day he was doodling on the back of his maths book when, suddenly, he had drawn his teacher's face. The other kids loved the drawing and all asked for one. Crimpy seized the opportunity to become an entrepreneur, charging sixpence for each cartoon he drew on one of the school's patter-tennis bats. Crimpy might have made his fortune had the headmaster not discovered his work on about 100 bats. His earnings were spent on sandpaper! He was not to be put off. He kept working at his cartooning until one day he bought a fax machine, set up a small studio and started 'annoying the shit' out of newspapers — 'and I just haven't stopped.'

Crimpy claims that he has grown up to become a human version of

Daryl Crimp (Crimpy) demonstrating his patented fish-measuring device which falls somewhat short on this catch, a snapper made by a friend from an old copper hot-water cylinder.

the ubiquitous Swiss Army knife. Over his eventful 42 years he has seized all opportunities, and had a crack at most things. He set out to become a helicopter pilot — until he ran out of money. He also became a schoolteacher but gave that away to 'become a real person'. He then took off on what he facetiously describes as 'an obligatory Kon-tiki brothel tour of Europe'. And, possessing a passion for storytelling, he is the author of several books, among them are *The Mad Chef*, and the *Wildfoods Cookbook*. The latter was launched at the 2000 Hokitika Wildfoods Festival, with a daring Crimpy demonstrating his own recipes. These days much of his income is derived from a daily deluge of stinging cartoons digitally propelled to a raft of mostly North Island newspapers and periodicals.

This much I knew about Crimpy before dropping in on him and his wife Annette Bormolini in their Nelson home. On arriving, I discovered that one more blade in Crimpy's 'Swiss Army' knife was revealed: he was about to become a father for the first time!

Wanting to know if Crimpy was a genuine South Islander, I asked if he would be happy living in Auckland.

'No way in hell,' was his immediate retort. 'I'm a country boy at heart. I grew up on a farm at Tadmore. Besides, I have just bought a bach in the Marlborough Sounds. And the fishing's great. I actually thought about moving there once. But, no. I love the South Island too much. And with computer technology I can make a living without having to be in Auckland. I choose to live here for the lifestyle. Everything's immediate. I get up in the morning, grab a cup of coffee, and I'm at work. Why would I change? Skiing in the Nelson Lakes National Park or fishing in the Marlborough Sounds are only an hour away. In Auckland it takes that long just to go and have a cup of tea with your mates, plus all the stress that goes with it.'

Annette is a fledgling South Islander. A recent import from Cairns, she speaks with a delightful Queensland twang. She came to New Zealand to meet someone in Motueka, but by the end of her first New Zealand winter a once promising relationship had run aground. 'I turned up in Nelson for a job interview on a perfect spring day and thought: This is it. I didn't brave the winter just to go home for a sultry summer.' She landed herself a bar job at the Rising Sun and one night she served beer to Crimpy who was visiting the hotel to attend a fishing club meeting.

Daryl Crimp and Annette Bormolini enthuse over their latest collection of fishing stories about to be let loose on a gullible public.

'I was about to leave when Annette turned up behind the bar. I thought she was rather cute so I stayed for a few more beers,' Crimpy remarked casually. 'A couple of weeks later we moved in together. A couple of months later we got engaged. A year later we got married. Another year later we decided to have a baby. We haven't mucked around.'

Annette looked proudly at her enlarged figure. 'All we ask for is a child that eats its crusts, and doesn't just grunt at you when you ask how it is. And it will need to have some manners.'

Crimpy and Annette were about to tour New Zealand's fishing clubs to launch the latest book, *Whopper Fishing Tails and True Fishing Lies*, and Annette was keen for me to know that the book's front cover, showing Crimpy with an impossibly huge fish, was no product of clever computer manipulation.

'It's a real fish,' agreed Crimpy with a grin. 'A 50-kg hapuka groper. It's the biggest bottom fish I've caught so far. I had to hold the fish up in front of about six photographers. They said, "For God's sake, Crimpy, look happy!" I managed to raise my arm and smile before I collapsed in a heap with the fish. It was a big fish. It was a whopper!

'It just took off like the Kingston Flyer when it was hooked. When it finally came on board an hour later, I could actually fit my head inside its mouth. I got my head halfway in and thought, no — it could still be alive!'

Crimpy enjoys writing about the characters he has met, and with humour. But he found selling humour to publishers was no joke. '"Humour doesn't work in this country," several publishers told me. I said, "Did you tell that to Barry Crump?" People have become so negative. It's almost a culture, as if being downtrodden is being politically correct. We have to be careful not to offend. It's obscene. What we all need is a damn good laugh.'

I had just uncovered another blade in the complex mechanism of this human Swiss Army knife: Crimpy was delightfully, and blatantly, politically incorrect.

The inspiration for writing had its origins when Crimpy, as a young teacher, was living in Westport. 'The old coal miners had a natural art of storytelling. On a Friday night in the pub I would sit in earshot of these old-timers. I was fascinated by their ability to tell stories. In the early days they had had a very hard life, with very little entertainment. So they would be in the pub of a weekend, and sit with their 7-ounce beers and be telling these yarns. A simple incident, with a little embellishment and creativity, became a wonderful story.'

As far as fishing yarns go, Crimpy merely says that some fishermen just get better at the embellishing. Fishing is probably one of the most natural attributes we all have; it goes back to our hunter and gatherer days. We are hunters of one sort or another, and it manifests itself in many different ways. 'Even an Auckland yuppie is still a hunter. When a yuppie is looking for the next job, or salary rise, he uses the same instincts, natural aggression and skills as were used by the cavemen.

'Fishing is one of the most accessible sports that everyone can enjoy to fulfil a natural hunting instinct. It's not like shooting, although I'm quite happy to go game shooting. But we've been brought up with a Walt Disney syndrome where animals have been given human qualities. Bambie is a cute cuddly thing, so anybody who shoots a deer is cruel. But it's okay to catch a fish. It's food for the table.

'Catching a big fish is a goal for many people. And there's always the opportunity to embellish the story about the one that got away. It's all part of the fun. I almost had this huge fish but it got away: it's a story of hope rather than failure. "I was there, and it was a bigger fish than anyone else had caught."'

Crimpy began writing fishing stories a decade ago for *New Zealand Fishing News*. Having had one story published, he was contracted to write a regular column.

'I had a month to come up with my next story. So I put the boat on the back of car, grabbed my father and we headed down to French Pass. We got two flat tyres on the way. Then, overnight, a stray cat ate the heads off all 57 pilchards we had for bait.

'Undeterred, we put the boat in water. I did the heroic slam of throttle as I put the boat in a big arc to go back to the wharf and, as the steering jammed, pulled all the cartilage in my shoulder. Two people were mowed flat as the boat ran aground.

'I managed to get the boat on the trailer to haul it out of the water. Then the car got stuck. Unhooking the car, the trailer and boat rolled back into the tide. Luckily I found this old Ferguson tractor under a tarpaulin. And the key was there! It belonged to a charter operator who was away on holiday.

'"If Danny catches you with that he'll kill you," locals told me. I replied, "That's all right, I'll have it back before he gets home. But nobody told me as I went down the ramp that it had no brakes. So that went into the tide as well.

'I couldn't get it started and some dry character tried to tell me it probably had damp points. The story just sort of evolved from there . . .

'From then on, there was some sort of disaster every time I took the boat out. I don't know if my perception sharpened or if God had a wicked sense of humour and he was toying with me, but the stories just keep presenting themselves.'

Crimpy has a rule. For any fish he catches, he always adds 2 pounds: apparently it's best to use the old imperial measurements when talking about the weight of fish. So if Crimpy catches a 20-pound fish, it sounds better if it's a 22-pounder. 'You can't tell from the photograph if it's a

Crimpy with his catches — snapper all over 20 pounds — from a secret fishing ground in the Marlborough Sounds. 'If I told you where I caught them I would have to marry you,' says Crimpy. (photograph Daryl Crimp)

20-pound or 22-pound fish. But if I obviously exaggerated and said it was a 40-pounder, anyone would look at photograph and say, "That's a load of bullshit, Crimpy!"'

He likes to tell the one about the fisherman who rowed his dinghy for two days through the Marlborough Sounds to reach a fishing spot. 'Once there, he caught this huge snapper. Fortunately he remembered to take a camera with him because he couldn't take the snapper back. Another two days later, back in pub, no one believed him until he dug into his wallet and pulled out this photograph. His mates were absolutely amazed. The photograph, alone, weighed 8 pound.'

Crimpy says everyone has a story to tell, even if they don't know it. Once he started writing he discovered its similarities to cartooning. Instead of a humorous picture with a pen and line, he drew it with words. 'I found it quite fascinating to draw a word picture in somebody's mind, and they would laugh at it.'

Soon we were talking about school teaching. Crimpy does not readily admit to this part of his career. 'My only defence is that I grew up, saw the light and became a real person. Collectively, teachers are boring people. I enjoyed the kids, on the West Coast, in Nelson and Marlborough, and in London, but teaching didn't challenge me. There was all the bureaucracy. You were put into a box. It was like Pavlov's dogs and that stifled creativity. I needed to be challenged all the time.

'But it was stressful to break from the comfort bubble of a regular salary. Suddenly I had to physically create my own income. After six months of panicking and learning all about rejection, I discovered opportunities were going past every minute. They were all there for the taking. Some turned out well. Others didn't. 'The smart thing is to get into areas where other people aren't working — and don't take holidays.'

Everything you do is a culmination of things that have happened in the past. 'Teaching wasn't for me. But the skills learned in teaching have enabled me to write a book for children. If I hadn't taken opportunities and made use of a broad range of skills, I would have been on welfare. Now I sometimes feel I'm running welfare.'

My first encounter with Crimpy had been during a phone interview before the launch of his *Wildfoods Cookbook*. His passion for cooking was to the fore as he claimed some of the best chefs have had no formal training. 'It's all about developing a natural flair for yourself.'

He had presented 150 easy-to-follow recipes using a variety of New

Preparing Roy's roast.

Zealand home-grown foods with rich, mind-blowing flavours. Some would be suitable for a gourmet dinner party but when Crimpy thought the book was becoming a little too serious, he added a recipe for a roast fillet of sandfly. 'I couldn't help myself. I was surprised it was taken seriously by the North Island publishers, and was included in the book,' he said. Other wacky recipes include typical Wildfoods Festival fare, such as curried huhu grubs, herbed huhu grubs and huhu grubs Indonesian.

While compiling the book he became involved with Monteith's brewer Keith Armstrong who suggested matching food with beer. 'I thought it was a joke. I didn't think he was serious,' Crimpy admitted. 'I haven't had much time for people who get carried away with wine tasting, and their so-called butterscotch or caramel flavours, and all the oak. I just taste wine.

'And I've never been a great beer drinker but I've become very partial to Monteith's. Monteith's also has appeal in that it's a South Island beer, brewed locally in a small Greymouth brewery. The upshot was that we sat down and cooked recipes, and matched the food to the particular varieties of Monteith's. It all turned out amazingly well.'

But preparing a recipe book had its difficulties. For Crimpy, a recipe should be only a guide and getting into the kitchen should be fun. 'You should let yourself go and experiment, because you can't come to too much harm. If you loosen up and gain a bit of confidence you'll be amazed by your results. And if a recipe requires a glass of wine, the remainder of the bottle should go into the cook. It helps to get rid of those inhibitions.

'My biggest difficulty was itemising things into tablespoons, teaspoons and other accepted recipe book measurements, whereas I worked in dollops or handfuls of ingredients. When I was writing the *Wildfoods Cookbook* Annette would follow me around my test kitchen and write down what I had put in.

'During the early days of our relationship she would tell me I had cooked something wonderful, but whenever she asked what I had put in, I could never remember. I had had a couple of glasses of wine, and had just thrown things into a pan.'

Annette also spends a lot of time enjoying the kitchen. But down at the bach the kitchen is Crimpy's domain. 'Nobody's allowed to cook there except me.' He talked with gusto about collecting a heap of scallops the previous weekend.

'We had some friends with us so I decided on something rich and sweet. I threw everything into a pan as usual, starting with some onions and a small amount of chilli, and a tiny amount of garlic to offset the sweetness and enhance the flavour. It turned out to be one of nicest dishes I've created. It had a zing without destroying the flavour of the scallops.'

While he was talking Crimpy had started cooking dinner. Roy's roast was on the menu, but if it was ever to be emulated I knew I would have to start note-taking quickly. Cooking, I was learning, was all about putting different ingredients together for a result.

In Crimpy's view, food has come a long way since he was brought up on granny's good old mutton roast. Roy's roast began as a Scotch fillet of ribeye with generous oriental seasoning. 'I was once a professional chef by default. Now, I'm a kitchen hobbyist,' Crimpy explained as he put together a potato kumara bake or 'something or rather'.

Somewhere in Annette's past is an Italian influence. 'That's one country where you can fully appreciate fine food,' Crimpy told me as he expertly entombed the meat in foil.

Crimpy offered me his last bottle of Monteith's Original and was soon entertaining me with raucous accounts of his cooking days which will be retold in a forthcoming book, *The Mad Chef Strikes Back*. Eventually Roy's roast was presented and we tucked in to the accompaniment of a fine bottle of red. Crimpy admitted that the meat had not turned out quite the way he wanted it, 'but the thought was definitely there'.

'The sauces aren't too bad,' said Annette cautiously. 'And Roy's roast is pretty good, too. Hey, we will have to do this again!'

'But we can't,' replied Crimpy. 'I've already forgotten the recipe.'

As we enjoyed dinner, Crimpy talked about interviewing the Naked Chef, Jamie Oliver, on Nelson's NewsTalk ZB where he does a food and fishing show. Even more memorable was the English chef Gordon Ramsay, known for the abuse he habitually throws around on such occasions.

'He was remarkably humble,' said Crimpy, covertly admiring his potato and kumara bake. 'I asked him what would he would prepare if he had to cook for me. And he replied, "Crimpy, if I had to cook for you I'd have to ask God what He had on the menu."

'He then went through this marvellous menu for an imaginary dinner party for his special guest. It was a very special moment.'

CHAPTER 17

REMEMBERING RUTHERFORD

Most people don't realise how marvellous, and how important, Rutherford's work with the atom was.

Gerald Tarrant

Almost a recluse, living in a semi-remote valley in Golden Bay, Gerald Tarrant lays claim to being the last person in New Zealand to have studied under Ernest Rutherford, the Nelson-born father of nuclear physics. That was at the University of Cambridge during the 1930s when Gerald was studying for his PhD at the famous Cavendish Laboratory. A close friend was the Australian physicist, Sir Mark Oliphant, also a Rutherford protégé, who died in Canberra, aged 98, just a few weeks before I caught up with Gerald Tarrant in August 2000.

When Gerald, who was born in Southampton in 1906, eventually retired after a long career as a teacher and lecturer in many countries, he chose the West Bank of the Motueka River. 'I spotted a farmhouse and knew I liked mucking around a great deal — painting, rebuilding, and that sort of thing. So 25 years went by happily enough until my second wife died not so long ago,' he said with regret. These days he has his small log cabin next to the home of his second wife's daughter, Susan, and her husband John Janke. The dwelling suits him — Gerald seems to fit. Despite his longevity, or because of it, his mind is as active as ever and he spends his days surrounded by books and scientific papers. During my satisfying afternoon with him I felt almost like a pupil with his ever-patient teacher, rather than an interviewer.

My interest in Rutherford had been sparked by two newspaper stories. One I wrote to promote the first touring exhibition, *Rutherford: The Story of a Kiwi Genius*, that paid tribute to the great New Zealander's life. The other was an obituary for Sir Mark Oliphant, who headed the team of British scientists who travelled to the United States in 1943 to

Aged 94, Gerald Tarrant retains vivid memories of his professor, Ernest Rutherford.

help develop the atomic bomb that was dropped on Hiroshima and Nagasaki in 1945, bringing the Second World War to an end. I was also curious about the so-called 'splitting of the atom' attributed to Rutherford.

According to the *Collins English Dictionary*, Rutherford is a 'British physicist, born in New Zealand', but Rutherford himself said, 'I am a New Zealander first, and a Britisher second.' He was more than that — he was a South Islander. Born near Spring Grove in rural Nelson in 1871 to hard-working Scottish parents, Rutherford became the most celebrated scientist of the twentieth century, picking up some 21 honorary doctorates from universities around the world. During his 42-year career he made three significant discoveries related to radioactivity and atomic physics, any one of which would have ensured lasting fame.

In 1908 his work with radioactivity earned him the Nobel Prize for Chemistry. Two years later his famous gold foil experiment determined the nature of the atom as having free space with a nucleus at the centre, laying the foundation for nuclear physics. Then in 1917 while 'playing marbles' with atoms he observed the conversion of oxygen atoms into nitrogen atoms or, as the newspapers reported, 'splitting the atom'.

He was knighted in the 1914 honours list and in the 1931 he was made Baron Rutherford of Nelson. When he died in 1937 the *New York Times* eulogy read: 'It is given to few men to achieve immortality, still less to achieve Olympian rank, during their own lifetime. Lord Rutherford did both.' His ashes are interred in Scientists' Corner, Westminster Abbey, close to those of Sir Isaac Newton, Sir Joseph (J.J.) Thomson and others. And an impressive outdoor memorial can be seen at his birthplace on the outskirts of Nelson city.

'Most people don't realise how marvellous, and how important, Rutherford's work with the atom was,' Gerald says. 'But New Zealanders are yet to take advantage of Rutherford's discoveries. For that, we should be ashamed of ourselves.'

For me, physics had always been a struggle, but it was not difficult to embrace the subject with Gerald Tarrant. Each question I asked was followed by a long silence before he delivered a carefully assembled answer with amazing logic and detail. He also had his theories about many things that 'needed to be thought about a little more rather than being dismissed'.

But what sort of man was Rutherford? In the exhibition I had written about he seemed too perfect — as a physicist and as a human being.

Rutherford is remembered on New Zealand's $100 bank note.

'Firstly, he was always loud,' Gerald began after a long deliberation. 'You would know he was coming before he got there.

'Secondly, he was always thoughtful of other people. But he would not tolerate slackness. He was a hard worker, and always occupied. He did a great deal of foreign correspondence, and he was a man of great influence. He corresponded with the Russian government and got into quite an argument over his famous student Peter Kapitza who had arrived at Cambridge's Cavendish Laboratory in 1921, having lost his family in World War I.

'Rutherford got a special laboratory built for him to do work on magnetic field production. But on one occasion when Kapitza went back to Russia, as usual, for a holiday, he was not allowed to return to England. My guess is that the Russian government thought Kapitza's work might have some connection with releasing energy residing in atoms.'

It was the young Russian, apparently, who gave Rutherford his famous nickname 'The Crocodile'. Among several versions of the story, Rutherford was said to be like the crocodile in James Barrie's *Peter Pan* — heard long before it arrived.

Gerald Tarrant took his first degree at Cambridge, then spent another five years studying for his research degree in gamma (electromagnetic) radiation. Rutherford called on him weekly for a quarter of an hour to check his work and the students were invited to Rutherford's home one Sunday each month for afternoon tea.

'We were told to arrive about half-past-three. We then spent quite some time shifting rather large stones in the garden under the supervision of Lady Rutherford. We'd be shifting them from one position to the next, and often back again the next Sunday. Then Rutherford would eventually come out and have afternoon tea with us. We were told he had been working inside, but everyone suspected he had been having his afternoon sleep!

'Even though we were young students and we were associated with Rutherford during the last years of his life, he never seemed old to any of us. He was a tall imposing man who always looked as if he was in the prime of his life.'

For Gerald, Ernest Rutherford was one of the few 'really great men' of the twentieth century. 'First of all in the early nineteenth century there was Michael Faraday, a bookbinder. He discovered electricity. Second, there was [James] Clerk Maxwell. He was a theoretician who cleared up

A bust of Ernest Rutherford, made from plaster with bronze paint by an unknown artist, is kept at Nelson College where Rutherford was head boy in 1889. (Photograph Roy Sinclair, courtesy The Press*)*

the laws regarding electromagnetism, and showed there was such a thing as electromagnetic waves.

'Third, there was J.J. Thomson. The first thing he did was to improve the devices to create a vacuum. He also discharged electricity in gases and that's the reason why we have radio today. It was the beginning of radioactivity. And he also discovered the electron — in 1897. It was the apparatus Thomson produced that Rutherford used for the rest of his life. Without it, Rutherford could not have succeeded.'

In 1895 he had elected to work with Professor Thomson at Cambridge's Cavendish Laboratory and later the New Zealander took over his teacher's work, which had left unsolved such mysteries as why radium would glow in the dark. Gerald has a great respect for Thomson who was awarded the Nobel Prize for Physics in 1906. 'It is interesting how the name "Thomson" pops up in science. There are a lot of Thomsons and Thompsons. Rutherford's mother was a Thompson. And my mother was a Thompson. But they weren't the same mothers!'

For his own research thesis Gerald Tarrant was checking the work of Paul Dirac, a young genius who shared the 1933 Nobel Prize for Physics. Dirac had proposed a completely novel approach to relativity in connection with the movement of high-speed electric charges such as electrons. Gerald confirmed that Dirac's expectation was correct, but he also discovered another frequency of X-ray (of double the energy) which Dirac had not anticipated. 'I knew my discovery was all in accordance

Statue of young Ernest at the Rutherford memorial, Brightwater on the outskirts of Nelson.

An interesting use for two of Ernest Rutherford's degree certificates awarded from the University of New Zealand. The lampshade is believed to have been made by a one-time neighbour of Rutherford. (Photograph Roy Sinclair, courtesy The Press)

with Dirac's ideas but it wasn't believed until about 30 years later, by which time all interest in it had departed. I believe this did my career a lot of harm.

Gerald Tarrant graduated with his PhD in gamma radiation at the time when 'the Jews were being bumped off in Germany and Austria'. Many of the Jews who were science graduates migrated to England. 'There were no jobs for a youngster like myself. I was not tested so why should they take on me when there were so many Jewish professors with so many more years of experience arriving in the country?'

Gerald took up teaching, becoming headmaster of a 500-pupil boys' school in Liverpool. He subsequently taught in Iraq, Pakistan, Thailand and Bangladesh. And somewhere in between, in 1948, he was appointed senior lecturer in the physics department at Canterbury University College (now the University of Canterbury). For a time he was in charge of the department following the death of Professor Chalklin in an air crash at Singapore. 'Quite rightly, I did not get the job as head of the department because I wasn't ready for it.'

Back when he was at the Cavendish Laboratory Gerald fell in love and decided to marry. 'I needed a wedding ring, but not a common garden variety gold ring. I wanted one that would last, made of platinum iridium. And I wanted, at least, a hand in making it.'

He managed to get his material from a London firm, Johnson Mattrey. It was a rod he could bend and spot weld together in the laboratory. 'I formed the ring and waited until the people had mostly left and pressed the button on the welder. There was a flash and all the lights in the department went out. The inch-diameter copper rods bringing the current to my ring had fused together, completely burying my ring.

'In due course we got the main fuses back. I sawed the copper rods to get the lump with my ring engulfed, and dissolved it in nitric acid. I then sent what was intended to be the ring back to Johnson Mattrey, telling them to do the job properly.

'My first wife wore it for 30 years until we stopped for a picnic lunch in a field of lovely white opium poppies. She took it off and forgot it. So if you happen to find a wedding ring beside a field of poppies, please remember it is mine.'

When he was at Canterbury University College, he had three children, and a job he liked, but he always needed to economise so he built his own house on Huntsbury Hill. While digging out the foundation he decided to enlist some extra help to shift the rock-hard clay. He placed some blasting powder, a fuse, some more powder, then clay powder and lit it, but the explosion had little effect.

'I started walking towards it, having decided it was a dud. But I then, instead, strolled off to get some lunch before setting it up again. BANG! The unexpected second explosion was tremendous. I was thankful I'd decided on lunch!'

Lady Rutherford had returned to Christchurch following the death of her husband, and lived for many years on the Cashmere Hills. Predictably, she invited Canterbury College students to afternoon tea when they would soon be helping her in her generous garden. In return, she would tell stories about 'Ernest'. When she died in 1954 Gerald Tarrant was one of the pallbearers at her funeral.

He departed from New Zealand in 1957 to take up a British government appointment teaching physics at a college of medicine in Iraq. He felt he owed some of his work to the country that gave him his education. It was to be for a short time, but he stayed away for 10 years, following a disagreement over paying tax in New Zealand while he was employed overseas. 'I knew I would have trouble just paying my hotel bill,' he recalls wryly. He finished his career teaching physics and maths in Pakistan and Thailand. In the meantime he had many scientific papers published, and he had written textbooks for mathematics and physics.

Like all natural teachers, Gerald Tarrant is a master at oiling the thinking processes and setting them in motion. He talks about genes. We are what we are because the genes in our primitive animal ancestors were frequently altered by the impact of flying high-speed electrons resulting from radioactive decays. Sometimes these were detrimental, but sometimes the changes produced were helpful. So gamma rays have produced the human race.

'Of course most sources of radioactivity have died away and ceased to exist. Surprisingly, it may be there aren't enough left to suit our bodies which may explain why, on average, Japanese living on the fringe of the nuclear bomb sites lived five years longer than normal.

'Personally I put my own longevity down to spending my five years of research in close proximity to a tiny portion of thorium C2 — about the size of a raisin, or a little smaller — which emits gamma radiation of 2.65 million electron volts of energy. It may well be that a little gamma radiation may do us good? You mustn't automatically assume it's wrong.' He also points out that married men get a little radiation if they sleep with their wives. 'And we know married men live longer than single men,' he says with a chuckle. (Gerald believes we must never automatically agree or disagree but think things out in a logical order or take a new tack.)

Gerald's theories have been borne out in the aftermath of the Russian Chernobyl disaster. It is now thought that those who were subjected to very low doses of radiation are not likely to suffer permanent ill effects; it is even possible that the experience will prove beneficial.

But the dropping of the atomic bombs on Hiroshima and Nagasaki also represent the world's greatest nuclear disaster. In Hiroshima alone, 75,000 Japanese died in two seconds, and over the next 50 years the death toll from radiation sickness amounted to an estimated 200,000. And Rutherford's work with the atom has irrevocably connected the New Zealand physicist with nuclear destruction, to the embarrassment of many of his fellow countrymen. Some mistakenly believe Rutherford invented the atomic bomb.

There is no doubt that Rutherford knew that tremendous energy could be extracted from the atom. But when he did his 1917 experiment, during World War I, he claimed it might be many years before the energy could be extracted efficiently. His personal wish was that the means of using the atom's energy would not be discovered until countries could live peacefully with their neighbours. Nuclear fusion, which made it possible to efficiently release energy from uranium was discovered in 1939, two years after Rutherford's death.

When I ask Gerald Tarrant's opinion regarding the relevance of Rutherford's work to the atomic bomb, my question is met with the usual long pause. Eventually he tells me that Rutherford's splitting the atom has a similar relevance to the invention of paper. 'If there had been no paper, no one could have drawn a plan and there would have been no atomic weapon. It is the same as saying, there was a long way to go from Rutherford's work to what happened in Japan.'

He then he goes on to question the notion that Rutherford split the atom. 'Rutherford did not make the atom split. He saw it split. He was observing when it shot off an alpha particle or a beta particle and changed from one atom to another.'

Gerald regrets that Japan and the West ever went to war, but an atomic bomb such as was used on Japan, or a nuclear disaster such as Chernobyl (caused partially by using out-of-date reactors), should not detract from the real issues of using nuclear energy, and its potential to save lives, even in New Zealand.

'Rutherford's work that gave the world its understanding of the atom with its vast amounts of energy was one of the most important things to ever happen. Our civilisation depends on energy, and in particular it depends on coal. Coal is needed to produce iron. Each year about 2000 people die getting coal from the ground. Then, thousands more die because of pollution caused by burning coal. Even in Christchurch people die from burning coal.

'On top of that is the argument that burning huge quantities of coal over many years, pouring carbon dioxide into the atmosphere, has warmed up the earth, and the sea. Warming the sea causes expansion of the water and subsequent flooding in many countries with possible great loss of life.' And this warming of the earth can lead to droughts in countries like Ethiopia, resulting in the deaths of millions of people.

'Rutherford's discoveries made the use of nuclear energy possible. It's the most important discovery by a long, long way. It's the salvation of the human race, and certainly of the living standards we have now.'

Gerald agrees that nuclear energy has its risks, as do motor cars. But continuing to burn large quantities of coal is also at tremendous risk. 'We want to balance out the advantages and disadvantages of the beneficial use of nuclear energy against coal. If you're going to remember disasters like Chernobyl in 1986 without taking into account disasters related to the mining and use of coal, then you are going to get cock-eyed.' He is adamant that even in New Zealand we should 'get rid of a silly fear of nuclear energy, and stop killing ourselves with carbon dioxide. We're still in the early days of nuclear energy, but we're in the late days of coal and oil.'

Gerald Tarrant's long life promises to finish remarkably close to where Rutherford's began. Gerald admires the way Rutherford struggled initially, and in this sense the physicist stands as a model for young New Zealanders.

Rutherford attended schools in the small rural towns of Foxhill and Havelock before going on to Nelson College where he was head boy and enjoyed playing rugby.

'But when he wanted a scholarship to go to a college of the University of New Zealand he succeeded only on his second attempt to get one

Rob Duff from Science Alive, in Christchurch, studies a model of Rutherford's nuclear atom.

of 10 scholarships offered nationally. He was lucky. He eventually graduated with three degrees from Canterbury College where he was influenced by the work of Professor Alexander Bickerton. He took a position as relieving teacher at Christchurch Boys' High School. But his teaching skills were such, his efforts to get a permanent teaching post went unrewarded.

'Then there was the question of going overseas. Again he failed when he submitted his work in 1893 for a scholarship. He tried again the next year and was accepted only when the chap ahead of him was unable to

Gerald Tarrant with Harley at his log cabin in Golden Bay.

meet all the conditions. Rutherford was the second choice so to speak.'

And again it was luck that enabled him to leave New Zealand in 1896 to attend Cambridge in England. But once he got there it was a different story. 'Rutherford was in his element. There was no more luck about it.'

In the 1920s when Gerald was about 14 he had heard and read about the possibility of sending radio signals so he decided to see if he could send a signal to his friend's house about half a mile away.

'First I had to make a transmitter, and that meant making a spark coil. I managed to get a mile of No. 40 gauge copper wire to wind around a bunch of iron wires.' He pulled out a hair from his head and studied it. 'The copper wire was about the same size as this,' he said, showing me the frail grey strand. 'I wound that coil, a whole mile, and I didn't get a spark. I knew my insulation had gone wrong. So I unwound it, and wound it again, taking greater care with my insulation between each layer. I still didn't get a spark. I tried a third time and then gave it up. I've never taken to it since. Had I had the money, I might have been able to buy one. I think I did well getting the wire.

'That coil is one that Rutherford would have needed for his work. He was lucky. Spark coils were beginning to be commercially used in motor cars about the time he first arrived in England. Later, Rutherford also had an extremely good lab assistant by the name of Everett. I remember him. He was a glass blower and could produce all the glass equipment parts that were required.

'After three years at Cambridge, when he was aged 27, Rutherford accepted a professorship at McGill University in Montreal, Canada. During that time he got his Nobel prize. From there he went to Manchester where he did his work on the atom. But he was really interested in the wireless. When he originally went to Cambridge he had the record for sending radio signals. He could send them about half a mile, from one house to another.

'Rutherford might have developed commercial wireless telegraphy instead of Guglielmo Marconi. But J.J. Thomson saw in Rutherford a researcher of considerable ability. So Rutherford gave the world an understanding of the nature of the atom.'

When I visited Gerald Tarrant I was taken across the Takaka Hill from Motueka by John Hurley, Mayor of the Tasman District Council. A big man in every sense, John has a passion for his district, and especially its history. 'We don't appreciate Rutherford in New Zealand as much as we should. I can imagine a small boy known simply as "Ern" growing up in nineteenth-century rural Nelson and having incredible ideas about things people would only know about in the future. I suspect he frustrated his practical parents with endless detailed explanations about determining the position of a thunderstorm, or the benefits of electricity, or what was to become known as radio.

'They would have sent the lad off to feed the chooks, or to do something else useful. And I have heard that some of his early school reports weren't all that good. He needed to pay attention, or take more interest in maths.'

How Rutherford had become one of the great twentieth-century scientists, having come from such humble beginnings in New Zealand's South Island has fascinated many people. I ask Gerald Tarrant, 'How did Rutherford do it?'

For the first time during the afternoon his answer is spontaneous. 'Fundamentally, it's Scotland that should be credited. It was jolly good, coming from a small place and from parents who were not wealthy. But Scotland is where his genes came from.'

CHAPTER 18

THE POSTMISTRESS

Visitors drive along the road thinking to themselves, 'Will it still be there?' And there it is. Just the same. It hasn't changed. It's just that much older.

Lorna Langford

On the last day of December 1993 Lorna Langford was still working as postmistress at Bainham, a remote spot — it could hardly be called a town — in the north-western corner of Golden Bay. This was despite the post office's official closing early in 1988, along with about 400 others scattered throughout New Zealand. Her manner was very much that of a postmistress. Her distinctive, almost musical, voice carried a ring of authority and she was even wearing a predictable 'I told you so' look as I went to sign her visitors' book. 'There,' she said, 'you thought you'd be the first person to sign that book in 10 days or more. As you can see, I've already had someone from Spain in today.'

The tiny Bainham Post Office is part of a delightfully antiquated corrugated-iron premises that includes a general store that still advertises Frosty Jack ice cream. The only obvious building seen in Bainham, it is the last store and post office on the way from Nelson to the Heaphy Track. A cubby hole in the wall between the post office and store provides the only means of communicating between the two facilities. 'With only one of us here I can check up if anyone is in the shop. It acts as a bit of megaphone. I can hear people talking in shop and I can use it to pass money through.' A black cat is sleeping in the cubby hole. 'Oh, that's Panda. She thinks it's built specially for her!'

Lorna admitted to some traditional post office services she could no longer provide. 'This week I've had to turn away a motor vehicle registration and a savings bank withdrawal,' she said sadly.

To outward appearances the post office has changed little since the

Lorna Langford, still very much the postmistress, working in her Bainham Post Office in 1993.

1950s. The receiver bureau sign remains on the door to the telephone room. Nearby is a complete set of mostly outdated New Zealand telephone directories. The old post-office clock graces one wall, a photograph of Queen Elizabeth II taken just after her coronation another. A prized relic is the VR post-office letter-box plaque admonishing customers to register letters 'containing COIN or other enclosures of VALUE'. Such letters not registered, it warns, will be registered and charged double fee.

'All the accounting part and the telephone services have gone, but the mails still come and go. I sell stamps, handibags and other postal stationery, but I lost about a third of my customers not so long ago when Bainham went onto rural delivery.'

The first Bainham Post Office opened in 1896, with the schoolteacher as postmaster. 'Not this one. This building is post office number two built around 1928.' An earlier building — until recently used as a storeroom — can be seen out the back; it was built about 1902. The original post office was at the end of John Bain's verandah. The district was then called Riverdale, but that name wasn't allowed. There was already a Riversdale down south. Milltown was then suggested because a lot of milling was being done here, but that name was too much like Milton. Finally the two first settlers, Bain and Graham, combined their names and, presto, there it was — Bainham.

'I actually had a Mr Bainham come in yesterday. He said he'd always been keen to come and see this place. His name was spelt with a Y. He was from Wales and told me almost everyone he knew with the name Baynham came from his part of Wales. Their ancestors had been marauders who had worked over the Wales border. He said he thought there was a bad connotation associated with his name.'

When I first set eyes on Lorna Langford she was sitting at the high authoritative counter of her old Bainham Post Office, eating a salad lunch. She seemed pleased to see me despite my reporters' notepad. 'Oh, you're a left-hander, the same as me.'

She was born nearby at Collingwood. Her mother arrived in Bainham in 1924 after a seven-and-a-half hour trip from Takaka, sitting on a load of chaff aboard an unsprung dray. 'My father was a contractor and, later, a farmer. My mother once said she had a four-year engagement because it took her that long to decide if she could live here in such isolation. She ended up loving Bainham.'

Lorna started in the post office in 1947, assisting her grandfather Edward Bates Langford, who spent 28 years as telephonist and postmaster. Lorna, who took over running the post office and store in 1952, has bettered her grandfather's service by many years.

She once had visions of a modern store and post office but was disappointed when she saw the proposed plans. She put them away in a drawer and promptly forgot about them, deciding to keep the old building with its Frosty Jack ice-cream sign. Frosty Jack, Lorna says, was manufactured in Lower Hutt and was popular throughout Nelson until the early 1960s. 'I actually left off selling Frosty Jack before the factory was demolished. Not because we didn't like it, but it was more difficult to get. I would tell people, "Sorry but there's no factory there now." It sounded as if it was their fault, not mine,' she chuckles. 'I would sell them Tip Top.'

She remembers the threepenny and sixpenny telephone calls when she first started working. The last public telephone call was made from Bainham about 1987 when Telecom 'peeled off the little exchange'. 'A boy arrived having just completed walking the Heaphy Track and wanted to call his parents in Germany to let them know he was okay. When it came to doing the account Telecom said, "Oh, you can't do those any more." I hadn't received any official word.'

When the post office was officially closed Lorna managed to retain her grandfather's old gold dealer's books (one is now her visitors' book), the clock, the red posting box — for a time that was replaced by a modern box — and the historic VR plate.

'People come in, and I say, "You're having a look at the VR plate, are you? It's a bit special. It shows that the post office was opened during the reign of Queen Victoria." I just kept that by the skin of my teeth, really. They came to replace it. Oh, I was telling someone about it the other day and I never finished my story. Never mind.'

'Anyway, it was very badly damaged, being outside and vandalised. But people knew about it as they passed through on their way to the

Bainham's store and post office has changed little over the years.

The restored VR plate is a prized relic at the old post office.

Heaphy Track. "Be sure to see it," they would tell other track walkers. One visitor was a herd tester from the North Island. She still visits occasionally but, just quietly, it's the VR plate she visits, not me.

'The chief postmaster came and offered to get it restored for me but unfortunately the post office wasn't going to play ball. He had to come back and say, "Sorry, no way will they do it." I contacted the Historic Places Trust. They said they could restore the enamelling and wording. I got back to the chief postmaster and told him. He said, "Well, don't send it to them by post. They're a thieving lot of rogues in . . ."

'Then one day someone arrived with a new brown plate. He said he would put it on beside the old one. I suspected he was really going to replace my VR plate. My niece was here working for me and I said, "Keep and eye on him, and if he starts to take it off let me know."

'He did, and she did. And I went out, and by this time it was in his box. I said, "What are you going to do with this?" He said, "I am going to take it with me."

'Next thing it was under my arm — firmly. I said, "No you're not." I told him how we were getting it restored and I could see he didn't altogether believe me.

'So I said, "Would you like me to phone the chief postmaster?"

Lorna with her red post box.

'He said, "Yes." I had never in my life rung a chief postmaster but I thought this was worth fighting for. I went into the phone room. I was put through to the Nelson chief postmaster but someone pulled the plug. I was about to start over again when I heard a vehicle driving away. I had called his bluff.

'In the end the post office did restore the plate for me. They told me to put it on with brass screws because it is very brittle, and put it inside. Next time I had a visit from that man (and it might have been to paint the post box) I said to him, "Come in and see the plate." He was very nice about it. It was just as if he and I had arranged to get this thing done. Maybe he had? It all resolved just nicely. He was what I would have called a dour Scot.'

There was a time when the postmaster, or postmistress, had some standing in the community, along with the policeman and schoolteacher. Lorna recalled children who were not always very polite. 'They would come in and say, "Gimme the mail." I got a bit fed up with this and I would say, "I beg your pardon" and I would get "*Gimme the mail.*" Sometimes this happened a few times and then they would add "PLEASE". They then got their mail straight away.

'Then one of our oldest residents came in and said, "Can I have the mail?" I just added, "please". He looked at me and I could have dropped through the floor, I felt so devastated. It had just become a natural thing for me to expect this little bit of courtesy from the children, but to do this same thing to this elderly gentleman? He roared with laughter and whenever he came in he always said, "Can I have my mail — *please*." It became a bit of a joke.'

In preserving the old post office and store Lorna has not only resisted change but also created a tourist attraction unlike any other in New Zealand. And her post office represents the pre-New Zealand Post era.

She can talk about the old-style mail bag with their resmeltable lead seals. 'You could turn them inside out, but you cannot do this with the newer padlocked bags and you can never be sure if you've got everything out.'

Repainting the old red post boxes was simple. 'Someone arrived, got out of his vehicle, stirred up the paint and did the job and they were away in perhaps 10 minutes. Then I got a fancy modern box with fancy diagonal stripes. No way could anyone unpack three tins of paint and slosh it on in a hurry. One colour would dribble down into the other colours. I saw nothing wrong with red boxes that everyone here and from overseas recognises. Luckily I got my old one back.'

The South Island's northern West Coast, a lonely inlet near Bainham.

These days her general store is likely to be selling T-shirts, postcards and other souvenirs, rather than groceries from bulk containers. She recalls the days when icing sugar came in 20-pound tins, ordinary sugar in 70-pound hessian bags, cheese in 30-pound cloth-wrapped rounds and vinegar in wooden casks.

Although some locals are still loyal customers, she cannot match supermarket prices. Ironically, much of her postal work is bulk loads of pamphlets going out to promote the larger supermarkets of Golden Bay and Nelson. Her store and the original post office out the back both have Historic Places Trust classifications. 'Regrettably, such classifications don't pay to keep the boards on the walls.'

Over the years she has not ventured too far from Bainham. An exception was in 1971 when her store belonged to the IGA chain. She won a trip, with 28 other IGA storekeepers, to tour Australia. 'Nobody went from a smaller place and a smaller shop, and nobody had as many contacts.'

Calling Lorna again towards the end of 1999 I was delighted to hear her voice, unchanged. She was still very much the Bainham postmistress. And things were still very much the same at her post office and general store, although her address now had a New Zealand Post code: Langfords Store, Bainham 7170, Collingwood, Golden Bay.

 'It's nice to have a special post code for my store,' she told me. But she could not guarantee its future. 'I think I'll be here for a while yet, but then I sometimes get up in the morning and say to myself, "I wonder if I'll make it today?" I'm not getting any younger and, thank you very much, you haven't asked my age yet. When you were here six years ago you asked how long I had lived here? And, you didn't get an answer!

'People still come from all over. Today I had visitors from Adelaide and Waiheke Island. More often than not, people have heard about the post office and store before they arrive. Sometimes they have been before. They drive along the road thinking to themselves. "Will it still be there?" And there it is. Just the same. It hasn't changed. It's just that much older.

'But we seem to be losing some wonderful characters who don't seem to be replaced. I remember about 30 years ago this farmer rushed in to collect a registered letter. He said, "I can't stop, my cow's choking." The registered letter was obviously more important than the fate of his cow!

'On his next visit I asked after the cow. He said, "What cow?" and I said, "The one that was choking!"

'He said, "Oh, she's all right!"'

As the millennium dawned, the Bainham post office and store, identified by one of New Zealand's last red posting boxes, was still resisting change and Langford's Store was still a popular stopping off place for those on their way to the Heaphy Track.

'People just about always ask me how long I've been here at the store. I'm a bit lazy with figures so I just tell them I started working for my grandfather in 1947. When it came to 1997, I didn't have to do too much working out.'

Bainham seemed the perfect place to finish my South Island wanderings. Not far from the old post office I could catch a glimpse of that other half of New Zealand — the North Island. I must get there one day. Maybe those North Islanders could put up a few good yarns too? And maybe they could talk about their own special places? But all that will have to wait for another day. Right now I have appointment further south to revisit a tiny mountain village where a mysterious old Scotsman, with an impressive nicotine-stained moustache, once told me his stories.

BIBLIOGRAPHY

Adams, Grace *Jack's Hut*, A.H. & A.W. Reed, 1968
Beckett, T.N. *The Mountains of Erewhon*, A.H. & A.W. Reed, 1978
Campbell, John *Rutherford, Scientist Supreme*, AAS Publications, 1999
The Dictionary of New Zealand Biography Volume Three 1901–1920, Auckland University Press/Department of Internal Affairs, 1996
McLintock, A.H. (ed.) *An Encyclopaedia of New Zealand*, Government Printer, 1966
McMillan, Ross 'Blue Jeans' *The Country Bloke and Other Verse*, Otago Daily Times Print, 2000
O'Brien, Brian F. *Kiwis with Gloves On*, A.H. & A.W. Reed, 1960
Pope, Diana & Jeremy *South Island Guide*, third edition, A.H. & A.W. Reed, 1981
Tripp, E. S. *My Early Years*, c.1915

Booklets:
Historic Blackball, compiled by the Blackball History Group, 1993